CROSS STITCH
A BEAUTIFUL GIFT

CROSS STITCH
A BEAUTIFUL GIFT

DOROTHEA HALL

A Storey Publishing Book

Storey Communications, Inc.
Schoolhouse Road
Pownal, Vermont 05261

The mission of Storey Communications is to serve our customers
by publishing practical information that encourages personal independence in harmony with the environment.

Published in the United States in 1996
by Storey Communications, Inc., Schoolhouse Road, Pownal, Vermont 05261

First published in the UK in 1995
by New Holland (Publishers) Ltd, 24 Nutford Place, London, W1H 6DQ
Copyright © 1995 in text Dorothea Hall
Copyright © 1995 in photographs New Holland (Publishers) Ltd
Copyright © 1995 in artwork New Holland (Publishers) Ltd
Copyright © 1995 New Holland (Publishers) Ltd

Editor: Emma Callery
Designer: Roger Daniels
Photographer: Jon Stewart
Charts: Sarah Willis
Illustrations: King and King, Claire Davies and Lizzie Saunders
Jacket design: Peter Crump
Editorial direction: Yvonne McFarlane
Storey Communications editor: Gwen W. Steege

Typeset by Textype Typesetters, Cambridge
Reproduction by Hirt and Carter (Pty) Ltd.
Printed in Malaysia

Library of Congress Cataloging-in-Publication Data

Hall, Dorothea.
    Cross stitch — a beautiful gift / Dorothea Hall.
        p.   cm.
    "A Storey Publishing book."
    "First published in the UK in 1995 by New Holland (Publishers) Ltd."—t.p. verso.
    Includes index.
    ISBN 0-88266-901-X
    1. Cross-stitch—Patterns. 2. Gifts.   I. Title.
TT778.C76H3487 1996
746.44'3041—dc20   95-46681
                                                                    CIP

CONTENTS

INTRODUCTION

Some of our most valued and endearing gifts are those which are spontaneously given. One of mine is a small card showing a small posy of flowers and 'Welcome dear neighbor' beautifully and simply embroidered in cross stitch.

When I first moved into my house some years ago we had a long power outage on the second night but, as I collect candle holders, I lit some of the candles and waited for the power to return. Thinking we would be without light, my elderly neighbor called with her one spare candle and when she saw how the house was lit up, we laughed. In the end, it was I who gave her extra candles to take back! A few days later, I received her little card which I still have and treasure to this day. No matter how small or inexpensive, a handmade gift carries with it a personal value that money cannot buy.

In this book, I have designed a variety of projects which I hope will make pleasing gifts for all occasions, concentrating especially on the home and family.

For beginners and children, I thought it was important to include a range of small to medium-sized pieces such as the window shade pulls, stuffed animals and napkin rings, which they would enjoy making in a reasonably short time. So often, larger projects appear daunting and the amount of time and thought involved in making them is the very thing that can take the spontaneity out of making and giving them.

On the other hand, we may wish to make more elaborate gifts to celebrate family events such as the arrival of a new baby or a special birthday, for example, when the time involved can be planned and given – and the gift can be truly described as a labor of one's love.

In making my own gifts, my main concerns are that they should be unique, beautifully made with great attention paid to detail, and carefully chosen for the recipient. Using these guidelines for this book, I also wanted to expand the concept of a cross-stitched project and, where possible, bring in other handmade embellishments such as twisted cords and tassels, cotton pompoms, cloth buttons and so on.

To give something of a fun element, I transposed some of my young granddaughter's drawings into cross-stitch patches (see the child's pillow cover on page 91), stood them on their sides and stitched them together with large herringbone stitches. I feel quite happy to include other forms of embroidery with cross stitching, especially where one enhances the other and the overall decorative balance is maintained. The greeting card sachet on page 105 is similarly stitched. The flap is cross-stitched and the main sachet is lined and quilted and the seams joined with insertion stitch. These are the finer details that genuinely make a gift unique.

Sequins and beads add their own special sparkle to a decorative motif and can be used in conjunction with cross stitch just like any surface embroidery. I had great fun adding beaded tassels to the drawstring of the knitting basket (page 25) and also hanging similar 'drops' of glass beads to the centers of the carnation motifs. On this particular project, I felt the linen background fabric needed 'lifting', so I stitched medium-size pearls between the motifs and smaller pearls around the gathered top. It glistened!

Linen is a particular favorite of mine – it is an attractive evenweave fabric with a tactile quality all of its own, and it mixes well with other contrasting colored fabrics. The homespun look of some of them teams well with coarser furnishing fabrics, as in the blue and white cushion and the tartan-bordered cushion on pages 29 and 57. Others have a more open weave and where a contrasting lining shows through, the color effect is significantly changed with pleasing results, as, for example, in the nightgown sachet and the greeting card sachet on pages 19 and 105.

In conclusion, I would like to say that in designing these projects I have greatly enjoyed the challenge of getting the balance right between the fabrics, motifs, colors, threads and other embellishments and knowing that if I thought the projects were a success, then they would also be as gifts and I would hope that, like my little 'Welcome dear neighbor' card, the gift would be cherished forever.

BEFORE YOU BEGIN TO EMBROIDER

⌒ MATERIALS

The list of materials required, which is given with each project, states the exact measurements of fabrics, cardboard, trims and so on. However, because some evenweave fabrics fray easily, an extra 3 cm (1¼ in) all around has been included to allow for handling and stretching in a hoop or frame if preferred.

⌒ THREADS

A separate thread list for DMC six-strand embroidery floss is given with each chart and, unless otherwise stated in the list, you will need one skein of each color. Obviously, for small areas you will use less than a skein so check before buying to see if you already have leftovers of the same colors that could be used.

⌒ ORGANIZER

Once you have got your project threads together, it is a good idea to attach them to a piece of cardboard for safekeeping. To do this, you will need a piece of stiff cardboard with holes punched down one side. Cut your threads into a workable length of 50 cm (20 in) and knot them through the holes, adding their shade number opposite, in the order of the thread list.

⌒ CENTERING YOUR DESIGN

Always begin your embroidery by marking the center of your fabric both ways with tacking (basting) stitches, as indicated by the arrows on the chart. Begin stitching in the middle of the fabric, using the center lines on the chart and the tacking (basting) threads as reference points for counting the squares and fabric threads to position your design accurately.

⌒ PRESSING EMBROIDERY

Remember when pressing your finished embroidery to place it right side down on a thick, clean towel. Using a steam iron, or a dry iron and damp cloth, press with up-and-down movements, to give it a well-raised effect.

FOR THE HOME

~

Sweet-smelling Sachets

The custom of placing little scented sachets in drawers and wardrobes goes back to the days when many garments were made from wool. It was thought that strong perfumes such as lavender and rosemary offered protection against the ravages of the clothes moth.

Happily, that problem does not exist to the same extent today – clothes can be protected with zipped covers, wool can be mothproofed, and garments are made from synthetic fibers and so on. However, I think there is nothing nicer than the beautiful sensation of wearing freshly perfumed garments. Old-fashioned lavender and rose petal fragrances are very popular, as are essential oils, which are so easy to drop onto a pretty sachet.

~

And I will make thee beds of roses
And a thousand fragrant posies.

THE PASSIONATE SHEPHERD TO HIS LOVE

Christopher Marlowe (1564-93)

Each finished sachet measures
10 cm (4 in) square

☞ MATERIALS
Two 25 cm (10 in) squares of red
   evenweave fabric, 28 threads to
   2.5 cm (1 in)
25 cm (10 in) square of plain,
   contrast-colored cotton fabric

Tacking (basting) thread
Tapestry needle size 26
Embroidery hoop (optional)
DMC 6-strand embroidery floss:
   see the thread lists opposite
39 cm × 25 cm (15 in × 10 in) rectangle
   of lining fabric
Potpourri, rose petals or loose
   synthetic wadding (batting)

Essential oils
Matching sewing threads
1 m (39 in) of contrast twisted cord,
   3 mm (¹/₈ in) thick plus two
   matching tassels, each
   7 cm (2³/₄ in) long

Chart A

	white
	3823
	727
	742
	3689
	3806
	600
	472
	3817
	964
	3013
	3816
	3814
	3011
	3811
	800
	340
	3746

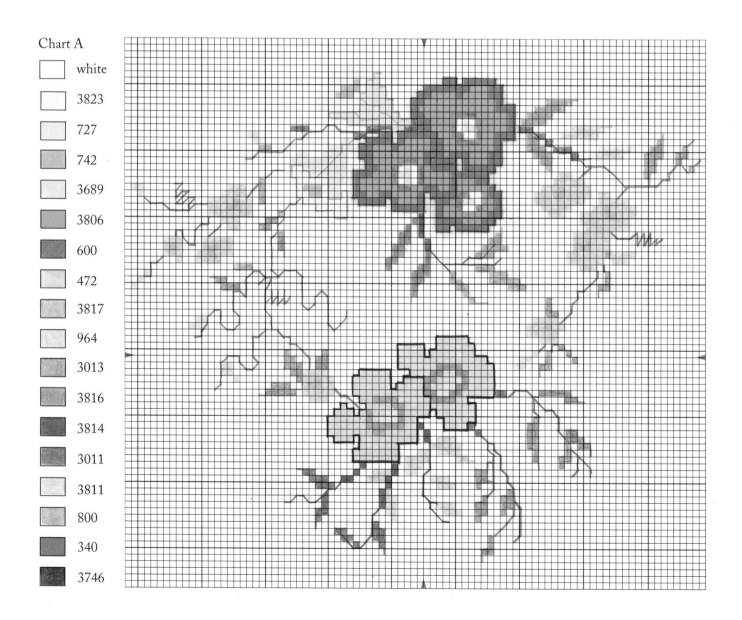

SWEET-SMELLING SACHETS

⌐ THREAD LIST A

	white
3823	pale yellow
727	yellow
742	deep yellow
3689	pale pink
3806	pink
600	deep pink
472	lime green
3817	pale green

964	pale viridian green
3013	pale olive green
3816	green
3814	viridian green
3011	olive green
3811	pale turquoise
800	pale blue
340	mauve
3746	purple

⌐ THREAD LIST B

	white
727	yellow
742	deep yellow
3689	pale pink
3806	pink
3811	pale turquoise
964	pale viridian green
3013	pale olive green
3814	viridian green

Chart B

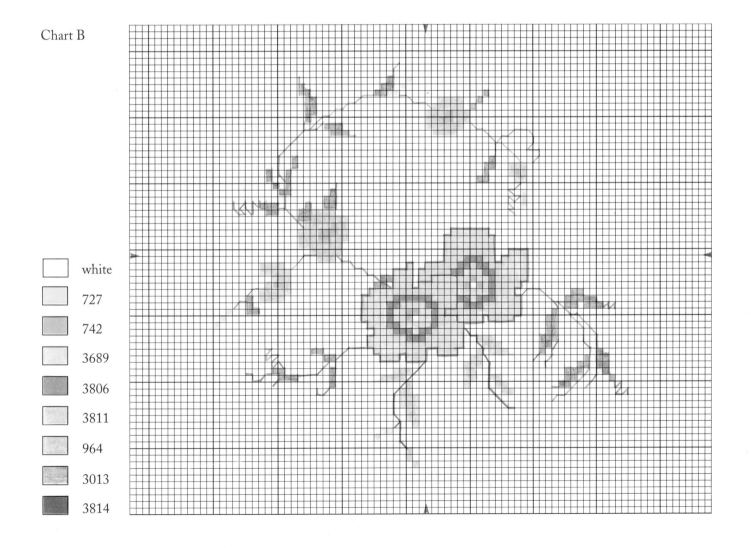

☐	white
☐	727
☐	742
☐	3689
☐	3806
☐	3811
☐	964
☐	3013
☐	3814

☞ THE EMBROIDERY

Both sachets are embroidered in the same way. Mark the center of your fabric both ways with tacking (basting) stitches. Work either in a hoop (see page 149) or in the hand, as preferred. Following the color key and appropriate chart, where each square represents one stitch worked over two threads of fabric, begin the embroidery in the center, using two strands of thread in the needle. Working outward from the center, complete the cross stitching and then the backstitch details.

☞ CHART A

Use a single strand of olive green 3011 for the flower stems, pale blue 800 to outline the freesia petals, purple 3746 for the pale pink flowers and deep pink 600 to outline the mauve-edged flowers.

☞ CHART B

Use a single strand of pale olive green 3013 for the main flower stems, viridian green 3814 for the two lower stems, and pink 3806 to outline the pale pink flowers.

☞ MAKING THE SACHETS

From the lining fabric, cut out three rectangles each measuring 13 × 25 cm

The folded sachet

(5 in × 10 in). Fold each piece widthwise in half, right sides together, pin and machine stitch around two sides, leaving one side open and taking 12 mm (½ in) seams. Cut across the corners and turn through to the right side. Stuff with potpourri, rose petals or loose wadding (batting) and add one or two drops of your favorite essential oil. Turn in the raw edges and slip hem the opening closed.

For the sachet covers, press the three main fabrics on the wrong side. Place one piece of embroidered fabric right side down with a scented cushion positioned centrally on top. The next stage is like wrapping a parcel. Fold the bottom edge towards the center, then bring the top edge over it and pin to hold. At the sides, fold in the corners and bring the

pointed ends in to meet in the middle of the back (see below). Overlap the points and stitch with a few oversewing stitches to secure.

Use the three sachets separately or tie the three together with a tasseled cord. Thread each end of the cord through the head of a tassel, pull the cord through and tie a knot at the

Back of sachet

end, so that it is hidden inside the tassel. Place the sachets on top of each other with the embroidered sides facing outwards and the contrast color in the middle. Tie the cord around and finish with a bow.

☞ ADAPTING THE BASIC SWEET-SMELLING DRAWER SACHETS

As an alternative to using potpourri or essential oils, you could, using the same parcel-wrapping technique and leaving out the inner cushion, wrap an exquisitely perfumed tablet of soap to give as a special present or to scent your own linen in drawers and wardrobes.

In the past, when good scented soap was scarce, new tablets were

Here's flowers for you;
Hot lavender, mints, savoury, marjoram;
The marigold, that goes to bed wi' the sun,
And with him rises weeping.

THE WINTER'S TALE

William Shakespeare (1564-1616)

SWEET-SMELLING SACHETS

always kept in drawers until they had dried out and become hard. In this way, the linen became beautifully scented, the perfume helped to protect against clothes moths, and the soap dried out and therefore lasted longer! These small, classic motifs are easy to work in gold with yellow highlights and, with their timeless appeal, would make an ideal gift.

The finished sachet measures 10 cm (4 in) square.

☞ MATERIALS
Two 25 cm (10 in) squares of cream evenweave fabric, 28 threads to 2.5 cm (1 in)
Tacking (basting) thread
Tapestry needle size 26
Embroidery hoop (optional)
DMC 6-strand embroidery floss: see the thread list below
Matching sewing thread
Two square or round tablets of perfumed soap

☞ THREAD LIST
972   yellow
        light gold thread
3032 brown

☞ MAKING THE SWEET-SMELLING SACHETS
Following the color key and charts given to the right and the instructions for the basic sachets, embroider the motifs finishing with the backstitching using two strands of brown 3032. Wrap the tablets of soap and secure each one as for the basic sachets.

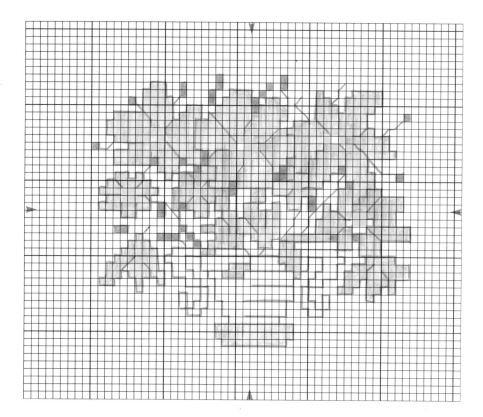

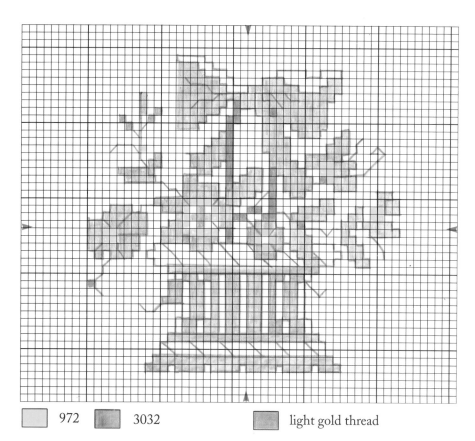

972   3032   light gold thread

NIGHTGOWN SACHET

A nightgown sachet instantly solves the problem of where to put night-clothes during the day. Prettily lace-edged and embroidered in a color to match your bedroom, use it to decorate the top of your bed along with other scatter cushions or, if you are making it for a child, along with her favorite dolls and toys.

I lined the sachet with a pale yellow lining but, should you choose a stronger color, you may like to add a white cotton interlining to prevent the stronger color from showing through the open weave of the linen.

~

I have spread my dreams under your feet.
Tread softly because you tread on my dreams.

HE WISHES FOR THE CLOTHS OF HEAVEN
W. B. Yeats (1865-1929)

The finished sachet measures
42 cm × 30 cm (16½ in × 12 in)
including the lace edging.

☞ MATERIALS
82 cm × 41 cm (32 in × 16 in) of
    off-white linen, 28 threads to
    2.5 cm (1 in)
Tacking (basting) thread
Tapestry needle size 26
Embroidery hoop (optional)
DMC 6-strand embroidery floss:
    see the thread list below
82 cm × 35 cm (32 in × 13½ in) of pale
    yellow cotton lawn for lining
90 cm (36 in) of off-white gathered
    lace edging, 5 cm (2 in) wide
Matching sewing threads
1.20 m (¼ yd) of bright yellow satin
    ribbon, 6 mm (¼ in) wide.

☞ THREAD LIST
725	yellow	3348	green
729	ocher		

☞ THE EMBROIDERY
Following the diagram given right,
mark the fold lines on the linen with
tacking (basting) stitches and, on the
sachet flap, mark the center both
ways. Work the embroidery in a hoop
(see page 149) or in the hand.

    Referring to the color key and chart
opposite, where each square represents
one cross stitch worked over two
fabric threads, begin the cross
stitching in the middle, using two
strands of thread in the needle.
Working outward from the middle,
complete the main motifs and then
add the backstitch details on top.
Cross stitch the outer border on three

Cross-stitched motif

sides, as shown on the chart, and then
add the inner line using backstitch.
Finish the border by tacking (basting)
the ribbon to the outside edge,
mitring the corners to neaten (see
page 155). Turn under the ribbon at
the top edges and, using matching
sewing thread, hem around on both
sides of the ribbon. Machine stitch if
preferred. Lightly steam press on the
wrong side.

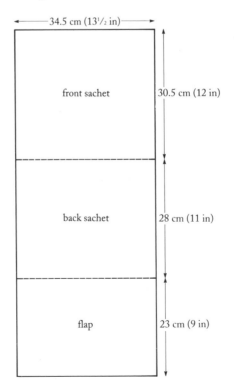

☞ MAKING THE NIGHTDRESS SACHET
Trim the embroidery to within
12 mm (½ in) of the ribbon border,
cutting around the flap and
continuing around the remaining back
and front sections, to measure
82 cm × 35 cm (32 in × 13½ in). On
the short side of the front section,
opposite the flap, make a single
12 mm (½ in) turning and tack
(baste) in place.

Lace edging on sachet

On the lace edging, turn under and
hem the cut edges to neaten. Lay the
lace on the right side of the
embroidered flap, placing the gathered
edge inside the seam allowance. Pin
and tack (baste) around. At the two
corners, allow a little extra fullness for
ease. With right sides together, fold
the front section so that the neatened
short edge is level with the flap fold.
Machine stitch around the sachet and
flap in one continuous movement. Cut
across the corners.

    On the lining, turn under and tack
(baste) the short edge, fold up the
sachet and stitch the sides in the same

[Diagram labels:]
34.5 cm (13½ in)
front sachet — 30.5 cm (12 in)
back sachet — 28 cm (11 in)
flap — 23 cm (9 in)

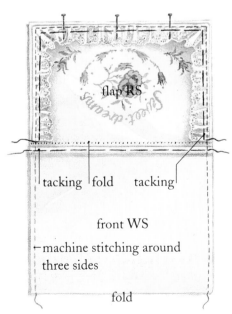

Attaching the lace edging

way as the main fabric. With right sides facing, place the lining and sachet flaps together, tack (baste) and stitch around three sides. Cut across the corners and turn the flap through to the right side. Turn the main sachet to the right side. Press all seams.

Slip the lining pocket into the main sachet, pin the top edges together and, using matching thread, slip hem to hold. Remove the tacking (basting). Add top stitching if preferred. Lightly press on the right side under a cloth.

☐	725
▨	729
☐	3348

Grey line indicates line of ribbon border

*Golden slumbers kiss your eyes,
Smiles awake you when you rise.*

PATIENT GRISSIL

Thomas Dekker (1572-1632)

Labels in image 2: flap RS, *Sweet dreams*, tacking, fold, tacking, front WS, machine stitching around three sides, fold

KNITTING BASKET

A pretty knitting basket embellished with embroidery, pearls and colorful beads makes an exquisite accessory. Useful and long-lasting, it would be the ideal gift for a special occasion, such as a major birthday coming of age.

As a young teenager I inherited a similar basket. It was very richly embroidered and sequined which, for some unexplained reason, I associated with the Far East. It suggested exotica, beautiful silks and precious stones, and it was all this that gave me the inspiration to recreate the image. I have decorated it with clusters of beads and dotted pearls over the surface but you may wish to add even more beads and sequins of your choice.

The mother, wi' her needle an' her sheers,
Gars auld claes look amaist as weel's the new.

THE COTTER'S SATURDAY NIGHT

Robert Burns (1759-96)

The finished basket measures overall 28 cm × 25 cm (11 in × 10 in).

⌒ MATERIALS

82 cm × 51 cm (32 in × 20 in) of antique white linen, 32 threads to 2.5 cm (1in)

Tacking (basting) thread

Tapestry needle size 26

Embroidery frame (optional)

DMC 6-strand embroidery floss: see the thread list below

Allow two extra skeins of each color for the twisted cord

Round basket 25 cm × 10 cm (10 in × 4 in)

1.2 m (1¼ yd) of lace trim, 4 cm (1½ in) wide

Pearl beads, small and medium sizes

Matching glass beads in various sizes

Matching sewing thread

Crewel needle size 9

Deep pink bugle beads

Small deep pink beads

⌒ THREAD LIST

3078 pale yellow
3822 yellow
3820 deep yellow
747   pale turquoise
598   deep turquoise
3811 turquoise
807   iridescent blue
772   pale green
913   green
581   olive green
962   pink
3805 deep pink

⌒ THE EMBROIDERY

Cut the linen in half to give two pieces 41 cm × 51 cm (16 in × 20 in). On one piece, mark a line across, 20 cm (8 in) up from the lower edge, with tacking (basting) stitches, and then mark a second line 18 cm (7 in) above. Within this 18 cm (7 in) area, mark the center both ways with tacking (basting) stitches. Work the embroidery in a frame (see page 149) or in the hand, as preferred. Following the color key and chart on page 26, where each square represents one stitch worked over two threads, begin the embroidery in the middle. Using two strands of thread in the needle and working outward from the center, complete the cross stitching and then add the backstitch details on top. Carefully press the embroidery on the wrong side and retain the tacking (basting) stitches.

⌒ MAKING THE COVER

Place the front and back sections together with right sides facing, tack (baste) and machine stitch the two side edges to within 12.5 cm (5 in) of the top edge, taking 2 cm (¾ in) seams. Press the seams open. Make a narrow double hem on each edge above the seams and stitch.

To make the drawstring channel, work on the wrong side and turn under 12 mm (½ in) on both top edges, then fold over a further 5.5 cm (2¼ in) and stitch close to the fold. Stitch a second line 2 cm (¾ in) above to complete the channel.

On the lower edge of the fabric make a narrow hem with the right sides facing and using a longer machine stitch for gathering. Pull up the gathers tightly to close the circle. This lower section forms the lining of the basket.

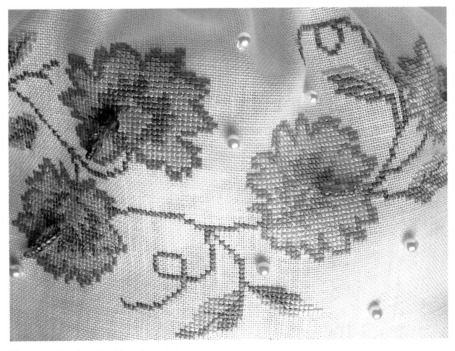

The completed embroidered motifs

Join together the raw edges of the lace with a narrow seam. Attach it to the right side of the fabric just above the lower tacked (basted) line. Place the pointed edge toward the top, tack (baste) and machine stitch in place.

Place the fabric inside the basket right side out and, following the tacked (basted) line, stitch the fabric through the canework just under the top edge of the basket, placing the stitches about 2 cm (³/₄ in) apart.

☞ ATTACHING THE BEADS
Using matching sewing thread, stitch a small pearl bead to the points of the lace (or every other point), and scatter medium size pearls at random over the background fabric in between the flowers (see page 152). Also stitch several to the back of the bag. Stitch small pearl beads to the top edge of the bag (above the drawstring) spaced about 3 cm (1¹/₄ in) apart.

Thread five or six glass beads and

Small pearl beads stitched to the top edge

attach them to the center of each flower. Begin by threading the smallest size bead onto a length of sewing thread. Move the bead into the center of the thread and then rethread the needle with the two ends to give a double thread. Continue to thread the remaining beads, working up to the

largest size. The bead at the end will hold the others secure.

Add clusters of bugle beads to the inner edge of the lace, holding it down so that the outer points fall over the basket rim. Attach a single deep pink bead above each cluster, stitching it carefully through the linen fabric only and not the lace.

☞ MAKING THE DRAWSTRING
Using three strands of embroidery thread, in a mixture of colors, make two twisted cords (see page 154). Each finished cord should measure 102 cm (40 in) between the knotted ends, but add a further 25 cm (10 in)

Beaded tassels

so that there will be 13 cm (5 in) of loose threads at each end on which to add beads in the same way as for the flowers. Before adding the bead 'tassels', thread the cords through the channel, as for the linen bag on page 35.

Glass bead drops

Clusters of bugle beads

Blue circles indicate approximate positioning for pearl beads

Cross patch,
Draw the latch,
Sit by the fire and spin:
Take a cup,
And drink it up,
Then call your neighbours in.

NURSERY RHYME

BLUE AND WHITE CUSHION

To see freshly plumped-up cushions filling chairs and sofas around the home is, indeed, a simple luxury, and instantly suggests comfort and relaxation. Perhaps this is a throwback to the past when ornamental cushions were a symbol of wealth and status. Today, however, we tend to choose the type of cushion best suited to the decorative style of a room.

Blue and white designs, such as the Chinese Willow Pattern and Delft tiles, have long been a favorite of mine and were the inspiration for this cushion. The cross-stitched sprigs of berries are offset with a deep border of bold blue and white checked fabric, which is also used for the back of the cushion. Two decorative bows secure the cushion closure at the center back.

Blue, darkly deeply beautifully blue,
In all its rich variety of shades.

MADOC IN WALES

Robert Southey (1774-1843)

The finished cushion measures 46 cm (18 in) square.

☞ MATERIALS

41 cm (16 in) square of white linen, 26 threads to 2.5 cm (1 in)

41 cm (16 in) square of white cotton for backing the linen

Tacking (basting) thread

Tapestry needle size 26

Embroidery hoop (optional)

DMC 6-strand embroidery floss: see the thread list below

60 cm (24 in) of blue and white checked cotton, 137 cm (54 in) wide

Matching sewing threads

33 cm (13 in) square cushion pad

☞ THREAD LIST

3747	pale blue	793	blue
		797	dark blue

☞ THE EMBROIDERY

Mark the center of the linen fabric both ways with tacking (basting) stitches. Then mark the center positioning lines for the outer four motifs by counting 51 stitches

(102 fabric threads) in each direction from the middle, and tack (baste) (see positioning diagram below).

Work the embroidery in a hoop (see page 149) or in the hand, as preferred. Following the color key

and chart on page 31, where each square represents one cross stitch worked over two fabric threads, and using two strands of thread in the needle throughout, begin the cross stitching in the middle with motif B. Complete motifs A and C following the positioning diagram given to the right. Work all the cross stitching and finish by adding the backstitch details on top. Lightly press on the wrong side if needed.

Trim the fabric evenly to measure 33 cm (13 in) square. This includes 12 mm (½ in) seam allowances,

which are used throughout the cushion cover. Using three strands of blue 793, and 6 mm (¼ in) long running stitches, stitch the grid lines between the motifs (spaced 10 cm [4 in] apart) and around the edge (see the positioning diagram below.)

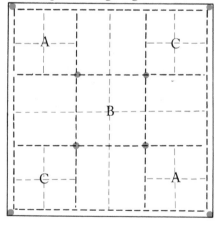

Positioning diagram

*T*ake thou of me smooth pillow sweetest bed,
A chamber deaf to noise and blind to light,
A rosy garland and a weary head.

SONNET

Sir Philip Sidney (1554-86)

ADDING THE TUFTS

Using blue 793, wind the thread around a pencil several times. Cut off, thread the end into a needle, wind twice around the threads and knot it

Tuft stitched on at marked intersection

securely. Remove the threads from the pencil and attach them to the cushion front at the intersecting points as marked on the chart. Cut through the loops, trim and flatten. Repeat seven more times.

MAKING THE CUSHION

From the checked fabric cut out the following: for the border, four pieces 48 cm × 10 cm (19 in × 4 in) and four pieces 33 cm × 10 cm (13 in × 4 in); for the backing, two pieces 33 cm × 22 cm (13 in × 8½ in); for the ties, four pieces 30 cm × 5 cm (12 in × 2 in).

On one back section, make a 12 mm (½ in) hem on one long edge. On the second back section, turn under 12 mm (½ in) and then 3 cm (1¼ in), stitch and press. To make the back opening, lay the back sections flat with right sides uppermost and the hems adjacent to each other.

Overlap the hems so that the deeper hem is below and the back measures 33 cm (13 in) square.

Make the ties by folding each piece of fabric lengthwise in half and stitch around two sides taking a 6 mm (¼ in) seam. Turn right sides out, and press. Attach the ties in pairs to the back opening, stitching them as in the diagram below and placing them 8 cm (3 in) in from the outer edge. Tack (baste) the overlapped edges of the back pieces.

To attach the border, place two of the shorter pieces on the embroidery, right sides together and with raw edges matching. Pin and stitch. Press the seams toward the border. Attach two of the longer pieces in the same way and press. Repeat on the back

Tied back of cushion

section. Place the front and back together with right sides facing and stitch around the edge. Trim across the corners, turn the cover through the back opening and press the seam. Stitch around the inside edge of the border through both layers, pressing the stitching through the previous line of stitches.

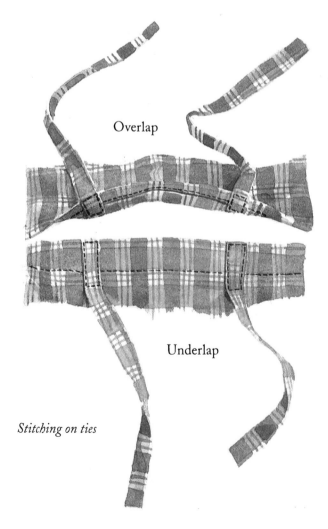

Overlap

Underlap

Stitching on ties

BLUE AND WHITE CUSHION

3747

793

797

● tufts

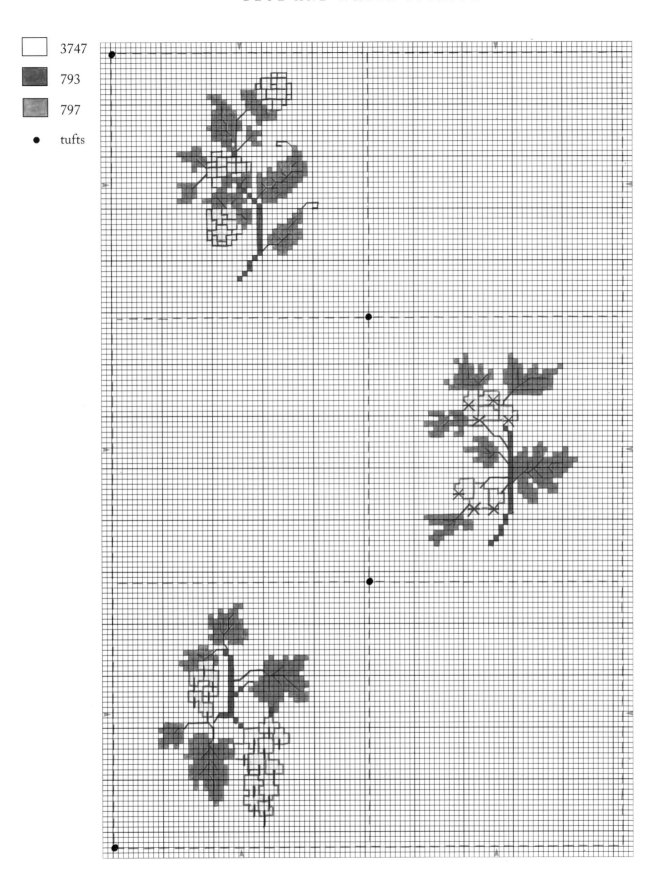

LINEN BAG

Even though 'linen' today has largely been replaced by cotton and cotton/ polyester, an Edwardian-style linen bag, such as the one shown opposite, makes both a pretty and practical accessory for any bathroom. Its roomy proportions will accommodate armfuls of laundry and with a simple drawstring top, it can be hung up behind a door, for example, out of the way. In my home, bags like this play a big part in helping to keep the bathroom and bedroom floors tidy.

The Edwardians may have edged their linen bags with hand-crocheted lace, but I've chosen to bind the edges with checked gingham, picking up on the crisp blue and white color scheme of the cross stitching. The central motif is a mock pocket flap complete with a large old pearl button and, to personalize the bag, I've added decorative initials, below.

~

Give me a laundry list and I'll set it to music.

Gioacchino Rossini (1792 -1868)

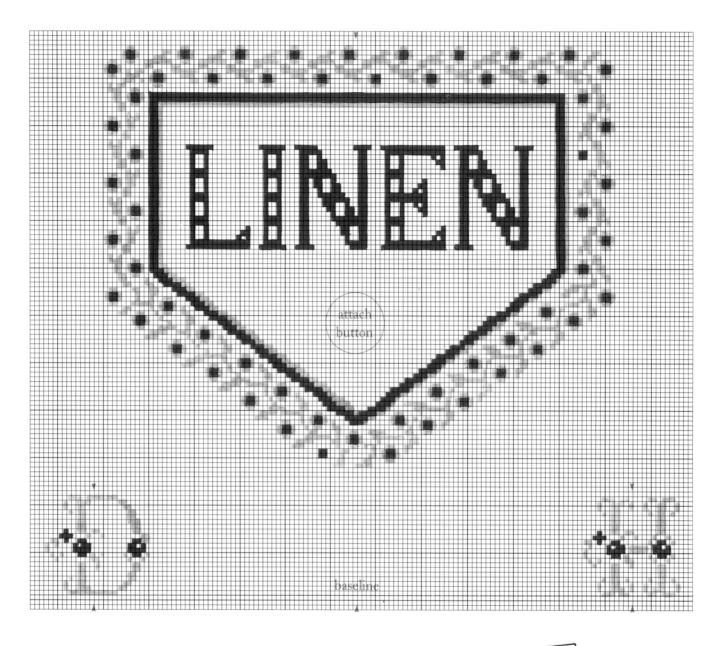

794

797

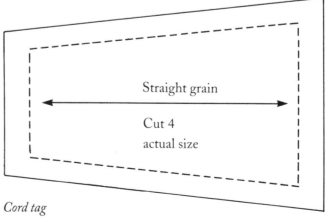

Straight grain

Cut 4
actual size

Cord tag

The finished bag measures 61 cm × 46 cm (24 in × 18 in).

⌒ MATERIALS
½ m (20 in) of white evenweave cotton, 25 threads to 2.5 cm (1 in), 142 cm (56 in) wide
Tacking (basting) thread
Embroidery hoop (optional)
DMC 6-strand embroidery floss: see the thread list below
Tapestry needle size 26
½ m (20 in) of blue and white checked gingham, 90 cm (36 in) wide
2.5 m (2¾ yd) of white cotton piping cord, size 3
Large bodkin
Large old pearl button
Matching sewing thread

⌒ THREAD LIST
794 blue   797 dark blue

⌒ ADDING YOUR OWN INITIALS
Following the alphabet given on page 141, first select your initials and then pencil in a vertical center line through

Cross-stitched initial

each one. To position the embroidery, match your pencil lines to those vertical lines drawn through D and H on the chart.

⌒ THE EMBROIDERY
Fold the fabric widthwise in half with wrong sides facing. With the fold at the bottom and using tacking (basting) stitches, mark the top layer of fabric (linen bag front) with a vertical center line placing the baseline 11.5 cm (4½ in) up from the fold, as shown on the chart. Work the embroidery in a hoop (see page 149) or in the hand, as preferred.

Following the color key and the chart, where one square equals two threads of fabric, and using two strands of thread in the needle throughout, work the cross stitching outward from the middle. Lightly press the finished embroidery on the wrong side. Trim the side edges evenly to 46 cm (18 in).

⌒ MAKING THE BAG
From the gingham check fabric, cut the following 6 cm (2½ in) wide bias strips: two pieces 76 cm (30 in) long and two pieces 25 cm (10 in) long. To neaten the edges before making the drawstring channel, bind both top side edges of the bag back using the 25 cm (10 in) long bias strips (see bias binding, page 153).

Working on the right side, and with the bag folded, tack (baste) the long bias strips to the side edges binding the two layers together in one movement, and stopping 25 cm (10 in) from the top edge.

Gradually ease away the back edge (which is already bound) and continue to bind the front edge only. Turn under the raw edges of the binding to neaten. Machine stitch.

To make the drawstring channel, fold the top edges to the wrong side to a depth of 10 cm (4 in) and tack (baste) to secure. Machine stitch a 2.5 cm (1 in) wide channel, placing it 6.5 cm (2½ in) below the top edge.

Made-up cord tag

Cut the cord into two halves. Using the large bodkin, thread each length through the channel starting from opposite sides. If the cord is too thick for your bodkin, knot the end, push a safety pin through it and use the pin to thread the cord. Knot the ends together. Cover each knot with two rectangles of gingham (see the diagram above). Turn in the edges and stitch around to neaten. Steam press the finished bag and attach the button using dark blue 797 thread, as shown on the chart.

$\mathscr{W}$INDOW $\mathscr{S}$HADE $\mathscr{P}$ULL

Recently, I bought an old Nepalese wooden bird, about 18 cm (7 in) long, with a hole drilled through the middle. Although the carving is primitive, the shape felt so good in my hand I thought it would make an ideal cord weight for the light switch in my bathroom.

Taking this as my inspiration, I followed the random movements of the carving for the cross-stitch embroidery, adding sequins to heighten the effect, and tiny strips of fabric for the beak and tail.

When stuffed, this simple triangular construction is easily shaped in the hand, and with a cord loop threaded through the body and secured with a large bead or two, it is transformed into a unique 'bird-in-the-hand' cord weight for your window shades or bathroom light switch.

$\sim$

$\mathscr{S}$weet bird, that shunn'st the noise of folly,
Most musical, most melancholy!

REFERRING TO THE NIGHTINGALE

John Milton (1608-74)

The finished cord weight measures
15 cm × 9 cm (6 in × 3½ in).

⌒ MATERIALS
20 cm (8 in) square of red Aida fabric,
    14 threads to 2.5 cm (1 in)
Tacking (basting) thread
Tapestry needle size 24
Embroidery hoop (optional)
DMC 6-strand embroidery floss:
    see the thread list below
8 cm (3 in) square remnants of red,
    yellow and dark green cotton
    fabrics
Matching sewing threads
Loose synthetic wadding (batting)
70 cm (27 in) of twisted cord in a
    contrasting color
Large bodkin
One or two large beads
Silver sequins
Small clear glass beads

⌒ THREAD LIST

3820	yellow	792	dark blue
471	green		ecru
3809	iridescent blue		

⌒ THE EMBROIDERY
Mark the center of the fabric both
ways with tacking (basting) stitches.
Work the embroidery in a hoop (see
page 149) or in the hand, as preferred.
    Following the color key and chart,
where each square represents one
stitch worked over one intersection of
fabric, begin the embroidery in the
middle. Use two strands of
embroidery thread in the needle and
complete the cross stitching first in
the upper triangle and then in the
lower one. Note that the motif in the

Those golden birds that, in the spice-time, drop
About the gardens, drunk without sweet food
Whose scent hath lur'd them o'er the summer flood;
And those that under Araby's soft sun
Build their high nests of budding cinnamon.

LALLA ROOKH THE VEILED PROPHET OF KHORASSAN

Thomas Moore (1779-1852)

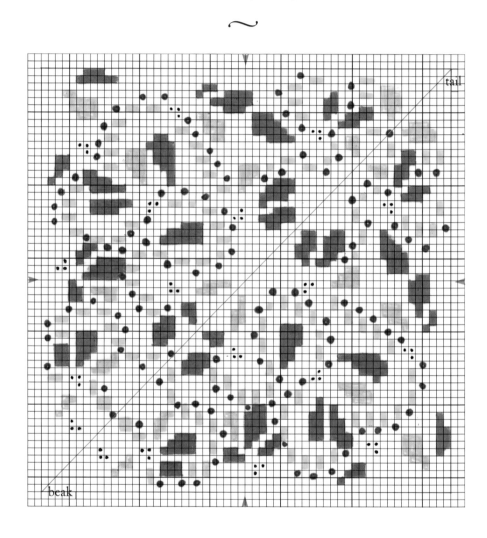

	3820
	471
	3809
●	792
•	ecru

*No human being, however great, or powerful, was
ever so free as a fish.*

THE TWO PATHS

John Ruskin (1819-1900)

~

second triangle is repeated in reverse.

Finally, using three strands of dark blue 792, work french knots to complete the design (see page 151). Lightly press the embroidery on the wrong side, if needed.

☞ MAKING THE CORD WEIGHT

Trim the edges of the embroidery so that it measures 13 cm (5 in) square. From the dark green cotton fabric, cut a 5 cm (2 in) square. Fold it diagonally across the middle and repeat. Press firmly. From the remaining pieces of cotton fabric, cut several pieces each 6.5 cm × 1 cm (2½ in × ⅜ in). With the embroidery right side up place the folded triangle in one corner, raw edges matching. Tack (baste) the tail pieces together at

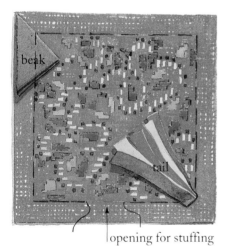

Attaching beak and tail

one end and place these in the opposite corner as shown in the diagram above. Tack (baste) within the seam allowance.

Fold over the embroidery diagonally across the center with right

sides facing. Pin and tack (baste) around the edges taking a 12 mm (½ in) seam and leaving a 5 cm (2 in) opening in the middle of the side below the tail. Trim across the corners and turn through to the right side.

Bird's beak stitched in place

Bird's tail stitched in place

Pull out the beak and tail. Stuff firmly with loose wadding (batting) using a pencil to help push it into the corners, and slipstitch the opening closed.

Working in the hand, make a birdlike shape by pressing the center back down and the head and tail upward. Then use the bodkin to add the hanging loop by passing the twisted cord up through the body and back down again, reinserting the bodkin in the same hole. Thread on one or two large beads and knot the

Beaded and knotted hanging loop

cords together. Finally, add the silver sequins, holding them in place with the small glass beads. For the eyes, secure the sequins with large dark blue 792 french knots (see page 151).

ADAPTING THE BASIC SHADE PULL

Continuing the idea of a diagonally-folded square of fabric, other animals such as fish fit equally well into the same triangular shape. Folded strips of fabric, for fins and a tail, are inserted into the seam in the same way as the bird's beak and tail. For the fish fancier, the tail could be extended in imitation of those exotic fish called veiltails, which have a large, flowing veil-like tail.

The finished cord weight measures 15 cm × 9 cm (6 in × 3½ in).

MATERIALS

20 cm (8 in) square of yellow Aida fabric, 14 threads to 2.5 cm (1 in)
Tacking (basting) thread
Tapestry needle size 24
Embroidery hoop (optional)
DMC 6-strand embroidery floss: see the thread list below
15 cm × 5 cm (6 in × 2 in) of yellow cotton
8 cm (3 in) square of red cotton
Matching sewing threads
Loose synthetic wadding (batting)
70 cm (27 in) of red twisted cord
One large bead
Two silver sequins
Two small red glass beads

THREAD LIST

| 741 | orange | 326 | dark red |
| 351 | deep salmon | 721 | dark orange |

■ 326   ■ 721   ■ 741   ■ 351

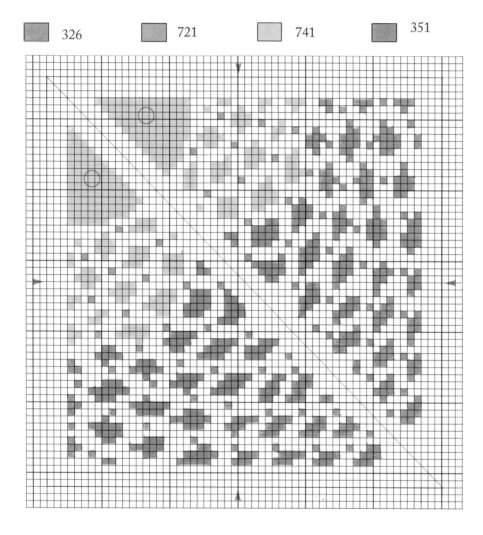

MAKING THE FISH CORD WEIGHT

Following the color key and chart given (left) and the basic instructions, work the cross-stitch embroidery. Fold the cotton for the fins in the same way as the bird's beak and tack (baste) in place. Fold the square tail fabric diagonally in half, pleat the pointed ends and tack (baste) in position, stitching the point into the seam.

Make up the fish as for the bird, adding the cord and finishing it by threading on the large bead and knotting the cord to secure. Work diagonal lines across the fins in stem stitch and deep salmon 351, if preferred. Stitch the sequin eyes in place, attaching each one with a small glass bead (see page 153).

ᖴish say, they have their stream and pond;
But is there anything beyond?

HEAVEN

Rupert Brooke (1887-1915)

SHELF EDGING

The practice of edging cupboard shelves with pretty embroidery or lace goes back to Victorian and Edwardian times when such things were fashionable. So much so, in fact, that even 'below stairs' pantry shelves were covered with paper (sometimes even newspaper) and the overhanging front edges cut with pretty scallops and notched patterns in imitation of lace or cutwork; and it was carefully redone whenever the paper needed changing. Today, shelf edging can be attached with self-adhesive pads, and is easily removed for cleaning. A pretty edging is eminently suitable for glass-fronted display cabinets and bookcases, or for kitchen dresser shelves where it gives a country cottage look.

~

Where's the cook? is supper ready,
the house trimmed, rushes strewed,
cobwebs swept?

TAMING OF THE SHREW
William Shakespeare (1564-1616)

The points of the finished edging measure 13 cm deep × 9 cm wide (5 in × 3½ in).

☞ MATERIALS

White Aida fabric, 11 threads to 2.5 cm (1 in); the total length of the shelf plus 4 cm (1½ in) seam allowances at each end by 18 cm (7 in) deep
Tacking (basting) thread
Tapestry needle size 24
Embroidery hoop (optional)
DMC 6-strand embroidery floss: see the thread list below
Ruler and pencil
White rickrack braid; the total length of the shelf plus 2.5 cm (1 in) seam allowances at each end, plus 28 cm (11 in) for each set of two points
Matching sewing thread
Self-adhesive pads

☞ THREAD LIST

321   red

☞ THE EMBROIDERY

Mark the center of the fabric both ways with tacking (basting) stitches. Work the embroidery in a hoop (see page 149) or in the hand, as preferred. Following the chart on page 44, where each square represents one cross stitch worked over one intersection of fabric, begin the embroidery in the middle. Decide whether the point or the inner angle should fall in the center of your shelf edging. You can quickly calculate how many points there will be by dividing the shelf length by 9 cm (3½ in). With even numbers, the inner angle

will fall in the center and with odd numbers, the point.

Using three strands of thread in the needle, complete the cross stitching, working outward from the center. Finish each single stitch with a reef knot behind and cut the ends fairly short. Repeat as required for any further shelves you might have.

Shelf edging with rickrack braid

☞ MAKING THE SHELF EDGING

Lightly steam press the embroidery on the wrong side. Lay it on a firm working surface wrong side up and, with a ruler and a pencil, lightly mark

the top edge and points as shown on the chart. Cut out. Snip into the angles, make a narrow single hem along the pointed edge: fold to the right side, tack (baste) and press. Pin rickrack braid over the raw edge and machine stitch through all the layers.

On the top edge, make a single narrow fold to the right side and press and apply rickrack braid in the same way. Using red embroidery thread, work a line of running stitches below the rickrack braid as shown on the chart. Turn in the side edges, making 12 mm (½ in) double hems and hem by hand or machine stitch to finish. Attach the edging to the shelf with the self-adhesive pads following the manufacturer's instructions.

What heart could have thought you?-
Past our devisal
(O filigree petal!)
Fashioned so purely,
Fragilely, surely,
From what Paradisal
Imagineless metal,
Too costly for cost?

TO A SNOWFLAKE
Francis Thompson (1859-1907)

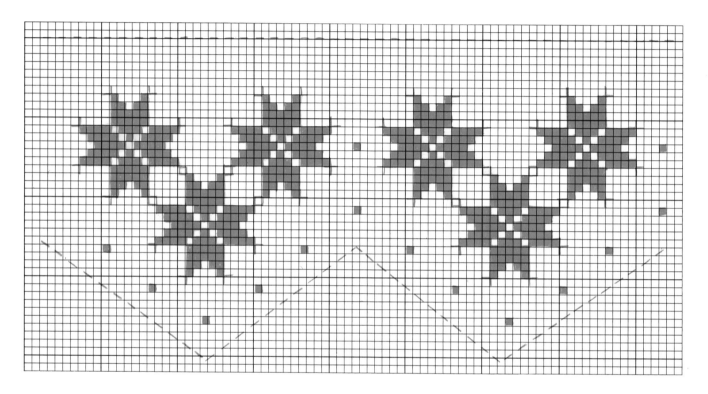

PLACE MAT

Mouth-watering fruits piled high on a decorative compote have long been the subject of artists and designers. Our forebears may first have painted them when fruit was plentiful after a good seasonal crop, and with justified pride, the fruit would be displayed as a dessert on dining tables and sideboards, in much the same way as we do today.

Worked on antique linen, the central motif is surrounded by a single border of running stitches in random colors and hemmed with open buttonhole stitch, also in random colors. The place mat would make a cheerful accessory when eating alone or, enlarged, it could be used equally well as a traycloth. Otherwise, repeat as needed to make a colorful set of place mats for all the family.

~

Ignorance is like a delicate exotic fruit; touch it, and the bloom is gone.

THE IMPORTANCE OF BEING ERNEST
Oscar Wilde (1856-1900)

The finished place mat measures 38 cm × 28 cm (15 in × 11 in).

⌐ MATERIALS

43 cm × 33 cm (17 in × 13 in) of antique white linen, 25 threads to 2.5 cm (1in)
Tacking (basting) thread
Tapestry needle size 26
Embroidery hoop (optional)
DMC 6-strand embroidery floss: see the thread list below
Crewel needle size 5

⌐ THREAD LIST

677   pale buff
3821 yellow
3827 peach
754   flesh
604   pale pink
760   pale brick red
961   dusty pink
606   vermilion red
3805 bright pink
3743 pale blue
3811 pale turquoise
3760 deep turquoise
472   lime green
907   bright green
3364 sap green
912   green
3810 deep iridescent blue
554   lilac
3746 purple

⌐ THE EMBROIDERY

Mark the center of the fabric both ways with tacking (basting) stitches. Work the embroidery in a hoop (see page 149) or in the hand, as preferred. Following the color key and chart on page 48, where each square represents one cross stitch worked over two threads of fabric, begin the embroidery in the center.

Using two strands of thread in the needle, and working outward from the middle, complete the cross stitching. Much of the charm of this embroidery is the colorful outlining, which is now backstitched on top. Using pale brick red 760, outline the pear, and then the apples, peaches and cherries with bright pink 3805. Add the pineapple details using sap green 3364 and the leaf veins with deep iridescent blue 3810.

Lightly steam press the finished embroidery on the wrong side and retain the tacking (basting) stitches.

⌐ MAKING THE PLACE MAT

Trim the fabric to measure 40 cm × 30 cm (15¾ in × 11¾ in), using the central tacking (basting) threads to cut both sides evenly. Hem the edges, folding 1 cm (³/₈ in) double hems. Press the folds, miter the corners (see page 155), and tack (baste) to secure.

A little peach in an orchard grew,-
A little peach of emerald hue;
Warmed by the sun and wet by the dew,
It grew.

THE LITTLE PEACH

Eugene Field (1850-95)

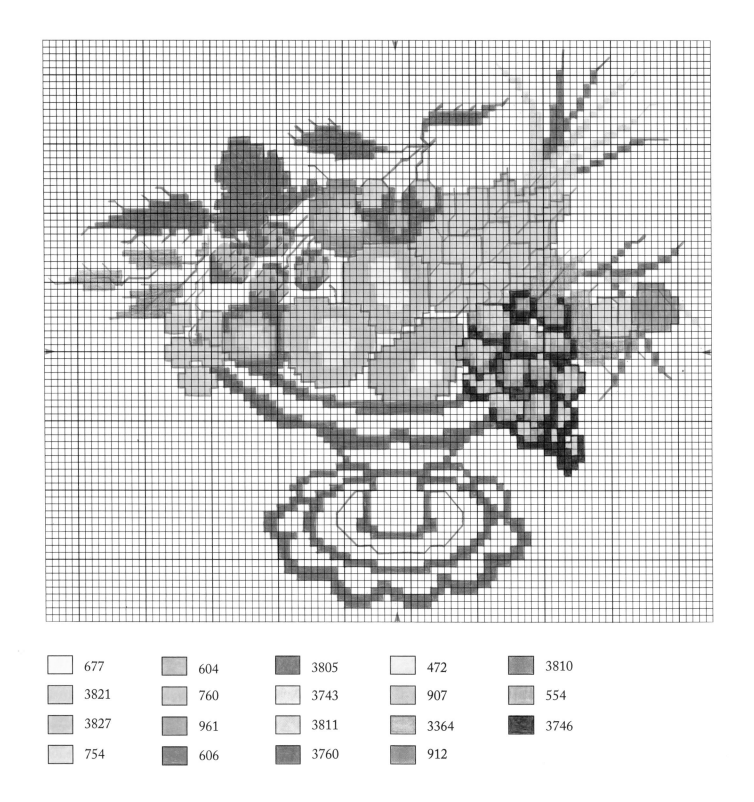

	677		604		3805		472		3810
	3821		760		3743		907		554
	3827		961		3811		3364		3746
	754		606		3760		912		

PLACE MAT

Using the crewel needle and two strands of embroidery thread, work open buttonhole stitch (blanket stitch) (see page 152) around the edges in random lengths of mixed colors—I chose some of the lighter colors from the fruit and leaves. Complete the embroidery with an inner border of running stitches, placed 2 cm (¾ in) inside the hem, again in random lengths and mixed colors. Remove the tacking (basting) and press on the wrong side to finish.

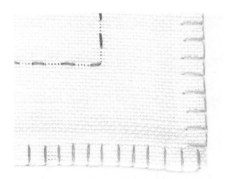

Blanket stitch around edge

☞ ADAPTING THE BASIC PLACE MAT

Simple fare! Succulent and juicy dessert apples and pears in a plain glass dish make a colorful partner for the basic place mat. Should you decide to make a set of place mats, why not embroider a mixed set using both designs. They would also make colorful pictures to hang in a dining room, or cushion covers.

Finish the edges of the place mat in the same way as the basic mat with random-colored buttonhole and running stitches.

The finished place mat measures 38 cm × 28 cm (15 in × 11 in).

☞ MATERIALS

43 cm × 33 cm (17 in × 13 in) of antique white linen, 25 threads to 2.5 cm (1 in)
Tacking (basting) thread
Tapestry needle size 26
Embroidery hoop (optional)
DMC 6-strand embroidery floss: see the thread list to the right
Crewel needle size 5

445	lemon yellow
973	yellow
743	chrome yellow
742	orange
977	burnt orange
352	pink
3706	salmon pink
606	vermilion red
900	brick red
891	red
3752	blue
472	lime green
3817	pale green
471	bright green
367	green
3012	olive green
3362	deep olive green
610	brown

☞ MAKING THE PLACE MAT

Following the color key and chart given overleaf and the instructions for the basic place mat, work the cross stitch and then the backstitch details, using three strands of blue 3752 for the glass dish.

Embroider the inner border and hem in random colors using running stitches and open buttonhole stitch, respectively (see page 150).

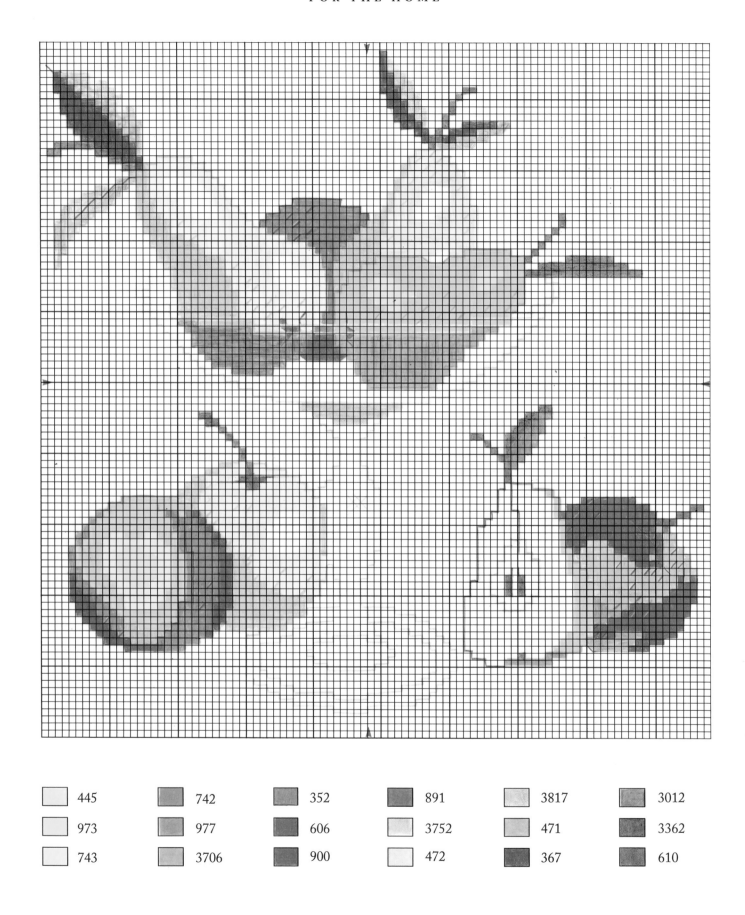

	445		742		352		891		3817		3012
	973		977		606		3752		471		3362
	743		3706		900		472		367		610

NAPKIN RINGS

The amount of embroidery needed for a napkin ring is just enough to encourage beginners to learn a new skill, especially children. As a child I enjoyed making them when I realized they could be made so quickly.

In next to no time, I'd made several in different colors for each member of my family. Soon, friends wanted them, and napkin-ring making almost turned into a mini-industry when my friends and I made and sold them for charity. Cross stitched in one color with a tiny button and loop for fastening – what could be simpler? You will see that the design can be worked in two ways: stitching either the motif or the background behind it.

~

The speech of man is like embroidered tapestries, since like them this too has to be extended in order to display its patterns, but when it is rolled up it conceals and distorts them.

Themistocles (C. 528-C. 462 BC)

The finished napkin ring measures
15 cm × 3 cm (6 in × 1¼ in).

☞ MATERIALS
Two pieces 23 cm × 12 cm
   (9 in × 4½ in) of white Aida fabric,
   11 threads to 2.5 cm (1 in)
Tacking (basting) thread
Tapestry needle size 24
Crewel needle size 7
Embroidery hoop (optional)
DMC 6-strand embroidery floss:
   see the thread list below
Two small buttons, 1 cm (⅜ in) across
Matching sewing thread

☞ THREAD LIST
349   red   310   black

☞ THE EMBROIDERY
Both napkin rings are embroidered in
the same way. Mark the center of the
fabric both ways with tacking
(basting) stitches. Work the

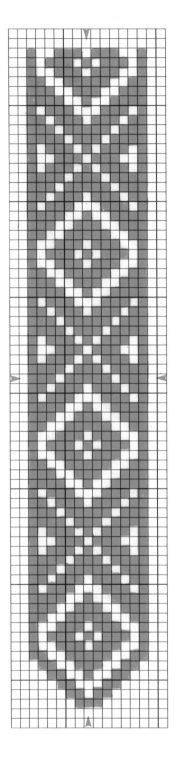

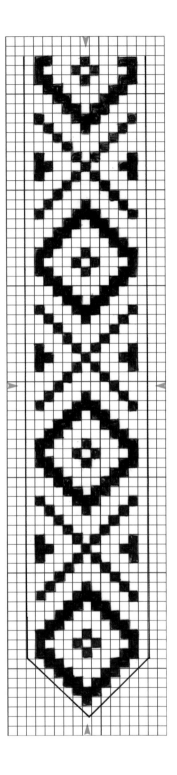

349

310

*And one of these strange changing
cloths was blue,
Wavy and long, and one cut
short and red;
No man could tell the better of the two.*

THE EARTHLY PARADISE. AN APOLOGY

William Morris (1834-96)

embroidery in a hoop (see page 149) or in the hand, as preferred. Small amounts of cross stitching, such as this, should not pull the fabric out of shape. Following the color key and chart on page 52, where each square is equal to one stitch worked over one intersection of fabric, begin the cross stitching, working outward from the center. Use three strands of thread in the needle and try to keep an even tension throughout. Complete the embroidery, remove the tacking (basting) and lightly steam press on the wrong side.

☞ MAKING THE NAPKIN RING

With the right sides together, fold the embroidery lengthwise in half and pin to hold. Tack (baste) across, one thread intersection away from the embroidery (see diagram 1, below). Note that on the black napkin ring, this should be two threads to balance the design. Measure the distance from the fold to the tacked (basted) line and mark this measurement above with pins. Using matching sewing thread, stitch across either by hand or machine. Trim the long edge leaving a 6 mm (¼ in) seam. Finger-press the

seam open and position it in the center of the embroidery, press flat (see diagram 2, below). Turn over and stitch around the point the same distance from the embroidery (see diagram 3, below). Trim the seam, cut across the corner and turn through to the wrong side. Trim the opening edges to 6 mm (¼ in), fold to the wrong side and slipstitch to close. Press on the wrong side. Using matching thread, stitch around the outside edges with running stitch, working close to the edge.

Sew on a matching button, as shown, and work a loop in buttonhole stitch (see page 150), in a matching color.

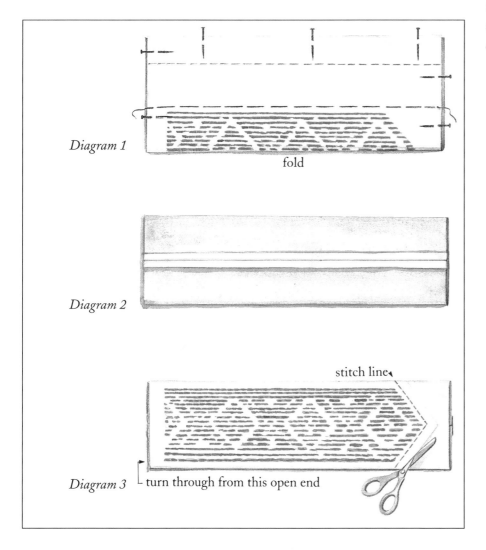

Diagram 1

fold

Diagram 2

stitch line

Diagram 3 └ turn through from this open end

TARTAN CUSHION

The color combinations of traditional tartans have a particular strength of design and vitality, and can be used in interior decoration as the main furnishing scheme to create stunning effects. This cushion, with its tartan border (and backing) could be used to great effect as a color accent on red, green, and gray furnishings, for example.

I chose this particular tartan, with strong reds and greens, so that when the colors were echoed in the cross stitching, they would show up well, but if your choice of tartan is different, simply replace the colors of the embroidery with those of the tartan. The cushion has a twisted cord trim similarly reflecting the colors of the tartan, but this is optional.

Mid pleasures and palaces though we may roam,
Be it ever so humble, there's no place like home.

HOME SWEET HOME

James Payn (1830–98)

The finished cushion measures
31 cm (12 in) square.

MATERIALS
28 cm (11 in) square of green/gray
   evenweave fabric, 28 threads to
   2.5 cm (1 in)
Tacking (basting) thread
Tapestry needle size 26
Embroidery hoop (optional)
DMC 6-strand embroidery floss:
   see the thread list below; plus one
   skein each of DMC 6-strand
   floss reds 347 and 814 for the
   cord trim
50 cm (20 in) of 90 cm (36 in) wide
   tartan cotton fabric
Matching sewing thread
33 cm (13 in) square cushion pad

THREAD LIST
347   red
814   dark red
943   viridian green
991   dark green
791   dark blue

THE EMBROIDERY
Mark the center of the evenweave
fabric both ways with tacking
(basting) stitches. Work the
embroidery in a hoop (see page 149)
or in the hand, as preferred.
Following the color key and chart,
where each square is equal to one
cross stitch worked over two fabric
threads, begin the embroidery in the
middle with the star. Using two
strands of thread throughout, and
working outward from the middle,
complete the embroidery. Lightly
steam press on the wrong side.

MAKING THE CUSHION
Trim the embroidered fabric evenly to
measure 24 cm (9½ cm) square. This
includes 12 mm (½ in) seam
allowances, which are used
throughout making the cushion cover.

From the tartan fabric, cut out the
following: for the border, four pieces
33 cm × 7 cm (13 in × 2¾ in) and four
pieces 24 cm × 7 cm (9½ × in 2¾ in);
for the backing, two pieces
24 cm × 15 cm (9½ in × 6 in); for the
tie, two pieces 30 cm × 5 cm
(12 in × 2 in).

Border stitched to embroidery

On one back section, make a 6 mm
(¼ in) hem on one long edge. On the
other back section, turn under 6 mm
(¼ in) and then 2 cm (¾ in), machine
stitch and press. Lay both pieces flat
with right sides uppermost (the
deeper hem below) and overlap the
hems so that the back measures
24 cm (9½ in) square.

To make each section of the tie,
fold the fabric lengthwise in half, right
sides together, and stitch around one

long side and one short side, taking a
6 mm (¼ in) seam. Turn through and
press.

Attach the ties centrally to the back
opening, stitching them inside the
placket (see Blue and White cushion,
page 30). Tack (baste) the overlapped
edges together.

Back of cushion with ties

To attach the border, place the two
shorter pieces on the embroidery with
right sides together and raw edges
matching. Pin and stitch. Press the
seam toward the border. Attach the
two longer pieces in the same way and
press. Repeat on the back section.
Place the cushion back and front
pieces together with right sides facing
and stitch around the edge. Cut across
the corners and turn through to the
right side. Lightly press, insert the
cushion pad and close the opening
with a bow.

To finish, using the red embroidery
threads 347 and 814, make and attach
a twisted cord to the outside edge of
the cushion (see page 154).

TARTAN CUSHION

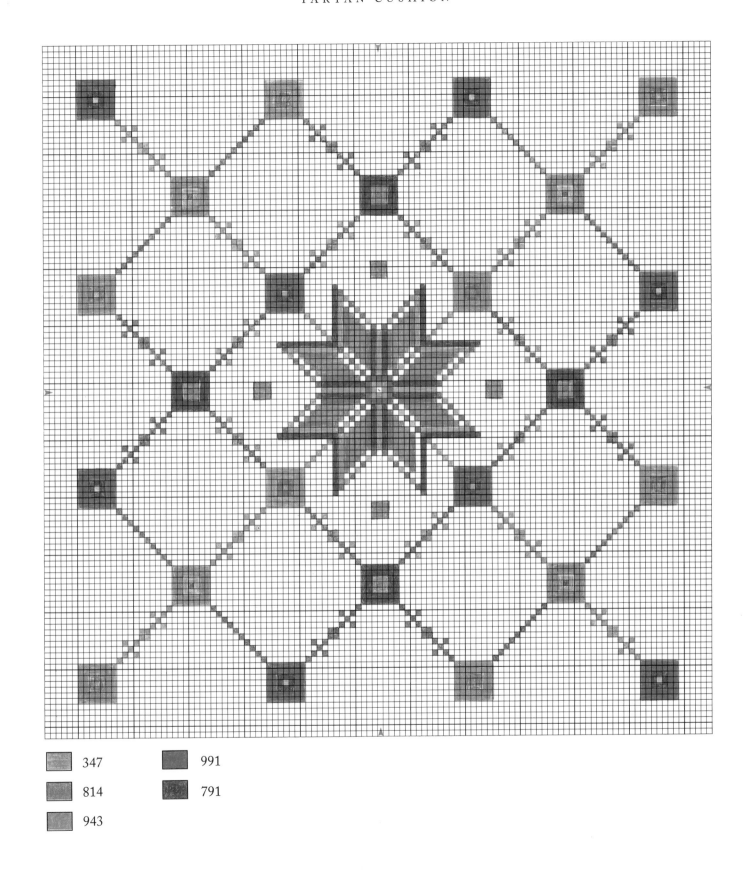

	347		991
	814		791
	943		

PRIMITIVE PAINTING

Inspired by the paintings of a group of amateur artists, who are primarily farmers, I decided to take a simply-painted picture of a family pet rabbit and translate it into a cross-stitch picture.

The original rabbit looked as though it had escaped from its hutch and was sittting in a well-tended, dark-colored flower bed. But, in its simply-stated outline, the rabbit also possessed a certain power and beauty that was immediately attractive—it had something akin to primitive art, a style of painting that has always appealed to me.

Meadows trim with daisies pied,
Shallow brooks and rivers wide,
Towers, and battlements it sees
Bosomed high in tufted trees,
Where perhaps some beauty lies,
The cynosure of neighbouring eyes.

L'ALLEGRO

John Milton (1608-74)

The finished unframed picture is 21.5 cm (8½ in) square.

⌒ MATERIALS

33 cm (13 in) square of deep red Hardanger, 22 threads to 2.5 cm (1 in)

Tacking (basting) thread

Tapestry needle size 26

Embroidery hoop (optional)

DMC 6-strand embroidery floss: see the thread list below

21.5 cm (8½ in) square of 3 mm (⅛ in) cardboard for mounting the embroidery

21.5 cm (8½ in) square of lightweight synthetic wadding (batting)

Strong thread or masking tape for securing the mounted embroidery

Picture frame of your choice

⌒ THREAD LIST

	white
	white
677	pale buff
676	buff
445	pale yellow
444	bright yellow
3820	yellow
741	orange
917	magenta
472	lime green
471	bright green
3012	olive green
993	viridian green
731	deep olive green

⌒ THE EMBROIDERY

Mark the center of your fabric both ways with tacking (basting) stitches. Then work the embroidery in a hoop (see page 149) or in the hand, as preferred. Following the color key and chart, where each square is equal to one cross stitch worked over two thread intersections, begin the embroidery in the center.

Using two strands of thread in the needle, complete the cross stitching, working outward from the center. Finish the rabbit before moving on to the flowers and then the outer border. In white, add the background spots and the highlight on the rabbit's eye. Then backstitch the details on top using three strands of deep olive green

The rabbit has a charming face;
Its private life is a disgrace.

THE RABBIT

Anonymous

731 to suggest the whiskers, and to outline the ears and the legs of the rabbit. Use two strands for the remaining backstitch details.

Lightly steam press the finished embroidery on the wrong side but leave the tacking (basting) stitches in place: they will be useful in centering the embroidery on the cardboard. Mount your embroidery ready for framing following the instructions on pages 155-6.

PRIMITIVE PAINTING

·	white
	677
	676
	445
	444
	3820
	741
	917
	472
	471
	3012
	993
	731

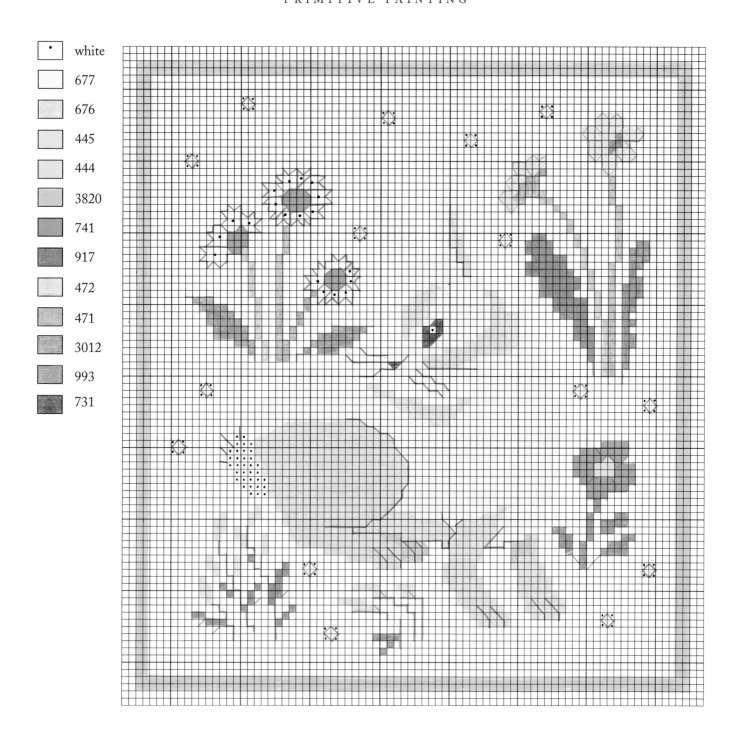

☞ ADAPTING THE BASIC PRIMITIVE PAINTING

In this picture, I have taken a small group of docile sheep under a horse chestnut tree and tried to capture the openness of the local farming area – the quietness and the loneliness. Although its simplicity would require an unfussy picture frame, I chose to echo red and green in a border of bias binding.

The finished unframed picture measures 21.5 cm × 20 cm (8½ in × 8 in).

☞ MATERIALS

31 cm (12 in) square of summer khaki Aida fabric, 14 thread intersections to 2.5 cm (1 in)
Tacking (basting) thread
Tapestry needle size 24
Embroidery hoop (optional)
DMC 6-strand embroidery floss: see the thread list to the right
76 cm (30 in) of red cotton bias binding, 2.5 cm (1 in) wide
23 cm (9 in) of green cotton bias binding, 2.5 cm (1 in) wide

Matching sewing threads
21.5 cm × 20 cm (8½ in × 8 in) of 3 mm (⅛ in) cardboard for mounting the embroidery
Double-sided tape for securing the mounted embroidery
Picture frame of your choice

☞ THREAD LIST

	white
743	yellow
606	red
817	dark red
813	blue
992	viridian green
367	green
318	grey
611	brown
310	black

☞ MAKING THE PRIMITIVE PICTURE

Work the embroidery in a hoop (see page 149) or in the hand, as preferred. Following the chart and color key given opposite and the basic instructions, work the cross stitching, using three strands of thread for the biggest sheep and two for the remaining cross stitch.

A flock of sheep that leisurely pass by,
One after one; the sound of rain and bees
Murmuring: the fall of rivers, winds and seas
Smooth fields, white sheets of water, and pure sky;
I have thought of all by turns, and yet do lie
Sleepless!

TO SLEEP

William Wordsworth (1770-1850)

Little boy blue,
Come blow on your horn,
The sheep's in the meadow,
The cow's in the corn.
Where is the boy
Who looks after the sheep?
He's under a haycock
Fast asleep.

NURSERY RHYME

Similarly, backstitch the biggest sheep using three strands of black in the needle, and the rest with two strands. Leave the background unworked. Lightly steam press the finished embroidery on the wrong side.

To apply the border, first cut one 23 cm (9 in) length and two 24.5 cm (9½ in) lengths from the red bias binding. Working from the wrong side, pin and stitch the bias binding to the top edge (see pages 153-4), raw edges even. Fold it over to the front and tack (baste) in place. Repeat this on the two side edges, turning in the short edges to neaten. Finally, add the dark green binding to the lower edge in the same way. Using two strands of green thread, secure the binding with even running stitches.

Mount the embroidery on the cardboard using double-sided adhesive tape. Place the tape around the outside edges, positioning the embroidery on top, and then press to hold. Frame under glass following the manufacturer's instructions.

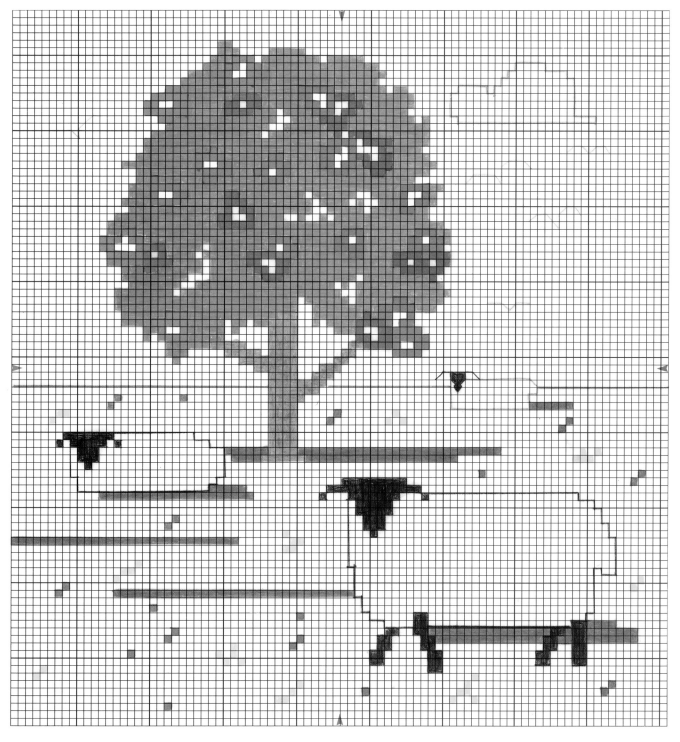

Bodies of 3 sheep, 1 cloud and centers of red flowers in tree are all stitched in white

white	606	813	367	611
743	817	992	318	310

FOR CHILDREN

BIRTH SAMPLER

The safe arrival of a new baby is always something of a miracle and has long been surrounded with traditions and customs. The day of the joyous happening, the date and time of the birth are all thought to influence the child's future and are precisely recorded in many different ways by adoring parents, family and friends.

Birth albums and printed cards are available for this purpose, but one of the nicest ways to mark the event is to embroider the baby's name and birth date (the time and weight, too, if you like), surround it with a pretty border like a sampler, and then frame it under glass. This can be given to the new baby or the parents as a special gift they'll be proud to display.

~

What's in a name?
That which we call a rose
By any other name
Would smell as sweet.

ROMEO AND JULIET

William Shakespeare (1564-1616)

The finished, unframed birth sampler measures 18 cm (7 in) square.

☞ MATERIALS

27 cm (10½ in) square of antique white linen, 32 threads to 2.5 cm (1 in)

Tacking (basting) thread

Tapestry needle size 26

Embroidery hoop (optional)

DMC 6-strand embroidery floss: see the thread list below

18 cm (7 in) square of 3 mm (⅛ in) cardboard for mounting the sampler

18 cm (7 in) square of lightweight synthetic wadding (batting)

Strong thread or masking tape for securing the mounted embroidery

Picture frame of your choice

☞ THREAD LIST

776	pink
3712	deep pink
3811	turquoise
472	lime green
563	green
470	olive green

☞ CHART YOUR OWN NAME AND DATE

Using a pencil and referring to the alphabet and numerals given on page 143, draw your own details in the spaces provided on the chart opposite, positioning them evenly as shown on the sampler.

Should the baby not have a second name, then move BORN and the date up and, in the space left between the date and the rabbits, work a fourth pink flower to balance the design.

☞ THE EMBROIDERY

Mark the center of the linen both ways with tacking (basting) stitches. Work the embroidery in a hoop (see page 149) or in the hand, as preferred. Following the color key and chart, where each square represents one stitch worked over two fabric threads, begin the embroidery working outward from the center. Use two strands of embroidery thread in the needle throughout. Cross stitch the border in the same way, working

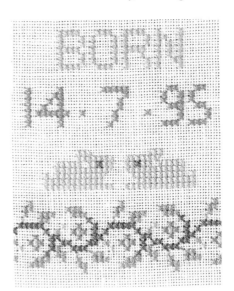

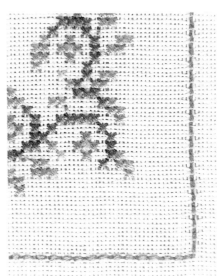

Sampler outlined with backstitch

outward from the center on each side. Using deep pink 3712, outline the sampler with backstitch working each stitch over three fabric threads, as shown on the chart.

Remove the sampler from the embroidery frame but retain the tacking (basting) stitches: these will be helpful in centering your fabric on the cardboard. Mount and frame the sampler following the instructions on pages 155-6.

~

I remember, I remember,
The roses, red and white,
The violets, and the lily-cups! –
Those flowers made of light!
The lilacs where the robin built,
And where my brother set
The laburnum on his birth-day, –
The tree is living yet!

I REMEMBER

Thomas Hood (1759-1845)

BIRTH SAMPLER

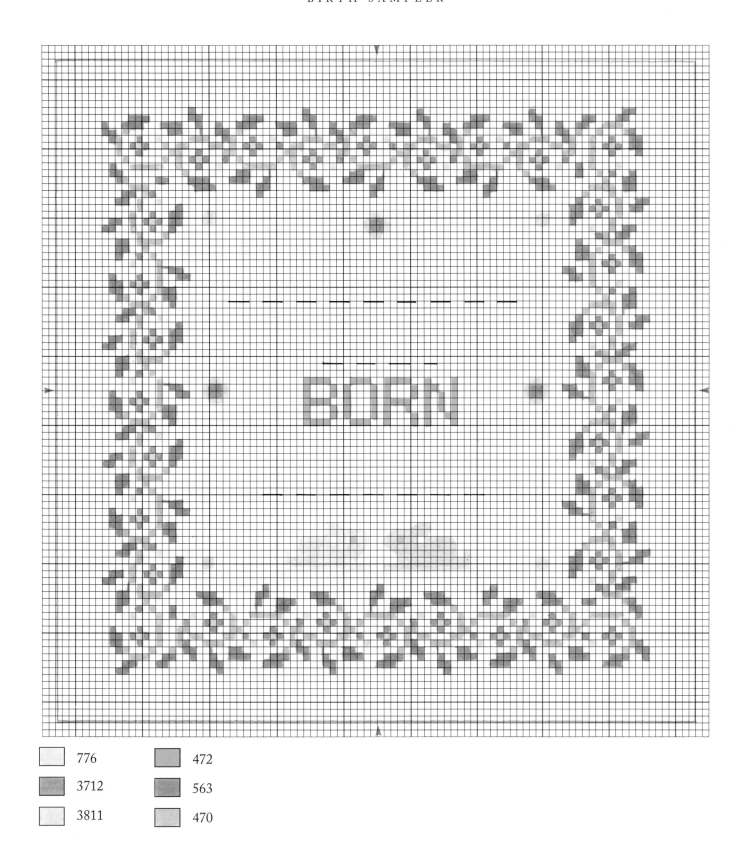

	776		472
	3712		563
	3811		470

STUFFED ANIMALS

Some of the most enduring toys of childhood are the simple, soft rag dolls and animals such as the teddy, cat and horse shown here. Often the cloth toys that do survive the rough and tumble of childhood have a worn, naive charm, which in itself, is greatly appealing and collectable.

These easy-to-sew stuffed animals are made in two pieces. Each animal is embroidered on one side only but you could, of course, embroider both sides, if preferred. You might also like to add a ribbon hanging loop, inserted into the top seam. I have made all three shapes fairly uncompli-cated so they can be stuffed to give gentle roundness to the toy. All three toys are quite soft to the touch, not too big for small hands to hold, and completely machine washable.

~

Sweet childish days, that were as long
As twenty days are now.

TO A BUTTERFLY, I'VE WATCHED YOU NOW
William Wordsworth (1770-1850)

Each finished hand toy measures
approximately 18 cm × 12.5 cm
(7 in × 5 in).

☞ MATERIALS
Six 23 cm × 20 cm (9 in × 8 in)
    rectangles of white evenweave
    fabric, 25 threads to 2.5cm (1in)
Tacking (basting) thread
Tapestry needle size 26
Embroidery hoop (optional)
DMC 6-strand embroidery floss:
    see the thread list below
Matching sewing thread
Loose synthetic wadding (batting)
Crewel needle size 7

☞ THREAD LISTS
Horse

3820	yellow	792	blue
833	ocher	648	gray
600	red	310	black

Cat

3822	pale yellow	900	deep orange
3821	yellow	3760	blue
783	ocher	310	black

Teddy bear

3821	yellow		
782	light brown	3814	green
922	orange	310	black

☞ THE EMBROIDERY
All the toys are embroidered and
made up in the same way. Two pieces
of fabric have been allowed for each
toy, and in each case, on one piece of
fabric, mark the center both ways with
tacking (basting) stitches. Work the
embroidery in a hoop (see page 149)
or in the hand, as preferred.

Following the appropriate color key
and chart (pages 75, 76, and 77),
where one square is equal to one cross
stitch worked over two fabric threads,
embroider the design working
outward from the middle, using two
strands of thread in the needle
throughout. For each toy, complete
the cross stitching and then work the
backstitch details on top still using
two strands of thread. Remove the
tacking (basting) stitches and lightly
steam press on the wrong side.

☞ MAKING THE TOY
For each toy, place together the
embroidered front and the backing
fabric, right sides facing, and pin to
hold. Allowing a 1 cm (³/₈ in) seam
allowance all round, cut out each
animal. Tack (baste) and, using
matching sewing thread, machine
stitch around the edge, leaving a small
opening for turning through and
stuffing. On the cat and horse, leave

3820
833
600
792
648
310

*B*etween the dark and the daylight,
When the night is beginning to lower,
Comes a pause in the day's occupations,
That is known as the Children's Hour.

THE CHILDREN'S HOUR

Henry Longfellow (1807-82)

the tail end open, and on the teddy bear, the head. Clip into angles and notch curved seams before turning to the right side. Press.

Lightly stuff with well teased-out wadding (batting) using the blunt end of a knitting needle to help push it into place. Turn in the edges of the opening and, using matching sewing thread, slipstitch to close.

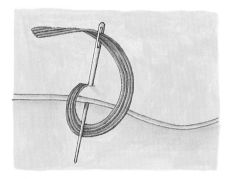

Stitching the horse's tassel

On the horse, knot several red 600 and blue 792 threads into the horse's neck, just below the mane. Using doubled thread in the needle, make a chain stitch through the neck seam (see diagram above), pull the stitch tight and cut the threads 2 cm (³⁄₄ in) long. Repeat as needed.

On the cat, attach whiskers as shown on the chart. Using two strands of black thread, backstitch the whiskers in place, cutting each one 2 cm (³⁄₄ in) long.

On the teddy bear, work at least four layers of straight stitches on the nose—to make it stand out—using three strands of thread in the needle.

3822		900	
3821		3760	
783		310	

3821
782
922
3814
310

ALPHABET BOOK

A baby's very first primer, this simple two-page book gives all the letters

of the alphabet cross stitched in bright red. Each capital letter is illustrated

with a friendly motif which, sooner or later, a baby will come across. I have

chosen the motifs for their sounds as well as their shapes. In my experience,

babies love to hear the names of things repeated over and over again!

The two pages are embroidered on both sides and have a fold down the

middle. The unfolded edges form the spine, which is simply bound with a

floral cotton lawn. This little cloth book is sturdy and completely wash-

able—an excellent gift for a baby's first birthday.

Babies do not want to hear babies; they
like to be told of giants and castles.

Dr. Samuel Johnson (1709-84)

The finished alphabet book measures 16 cm (6¼ in) square.

☞ MATERIALS
Two 36 cm × 20 cm (14 in × 8 in)
    rectangles of off-white Aida,
    14 intersections to 2.5 cm (1 in)
Tacking (basting) thread
Tapestry needle size 24
Embroidery hoop (optional)
DMC 6-strand embroidery floss:
    see the thread list below
Matching sewing threads
20 cm (8 in) of floral print strip,
    5 cm (2 in) wide

☞ THREAD LIST

	white
725	yellow
783	ocher
741	orange
351	red
600	deep pink
907	bright green
905	green
3753	pale gray
813	blue
648	gray
646	dark gray
676	buff
610	brown
310	black

☞ THE EMBROIDERY
You will see that the four pages are made up in two pairs, and each pair of pages is embroidered on the same piece of fabric. This has a center fold which forms the outside edge of the page. On each piece of fabric, mark the center horizontally and then outline the pages including the center

fold, and the vertical centers of each page, as shown on the chart and using tacking (basting) stitches.

Following the color key and charts (pages 82-5), where each square is equal to one cross stitch worked over one fabric intersection, begin in the middle starting with the letter E.

Ice cream with outlined details

Using three strands of embroidery thread in the needle, continue to embroider the letters, backstitching the appropriate parts of each letter as you go. Complete the cross stitching of the picture motifs, using three strands of thread, and then add the backstitch details last. Using a single strand of black 310, suggest the eyes

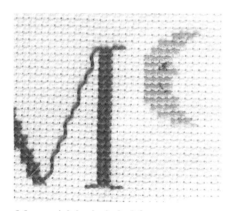

Moon with backstitched features

Outlined kite struts

and noses of the animals with a french knot (see page 151).

Embroider the second page in the same way, using a single strand of blue 813 to outline the ice cream and jug; black 310 for the kite struts and the french knots on the lion and orange base; and finally gray 648 for the moon's features.

Lion with french knots

Following the appropriate charts, embroider the third and fourth pages in the same way. Add the animals' eyes using a single strand of black 310, to make french knots and also the watch face details and the key supports on the xylophone. Use two strands of black for the stripes on the mother zebra, except for the neck and

Watch with added face details

head, which should be single. The baby zebra is outlined with two strands, but the inner body markings are all backstitched with a single strand. Retain the tacking (basting) stitches and press the finished embroidery on the wrong side.

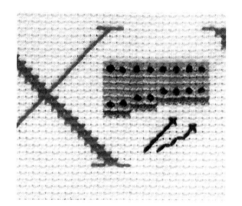

Added xylophone key supports

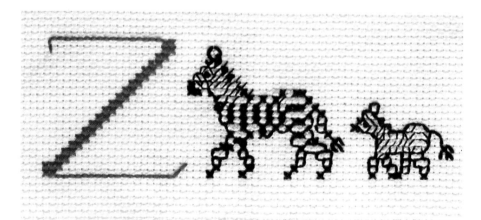

Baby zebra with outlined body markings

The made-up book with bias binding along the raw edges

☞ MAKING THE BOOK
On each double page, trim the two long sides to two thread intersections and the short sides to five intersections outside the tacked (basted) lines. Fold each double page along the center, right sides out, press and tack (baste) around. Using matching thread, zigzag stitch along the raw edges close to the tacked (basted) lines. Place the two folded pages together with raw edges matching and tack (baste) along the left-hand edge through all layers.

Bind the raw edge with the floral print strip. Fold it in half, right sides out, and with raw edges together, pin and tack (baste) it to the book front. Machine stitch, fold in the raw edges of the short sides and fold the strip to the back of the book. Pin, tack (baste) and hand stitch in place. Take out all tacking (basting) threads.

Elephants' tusks, central cross of flag, windows for house are stitched in white

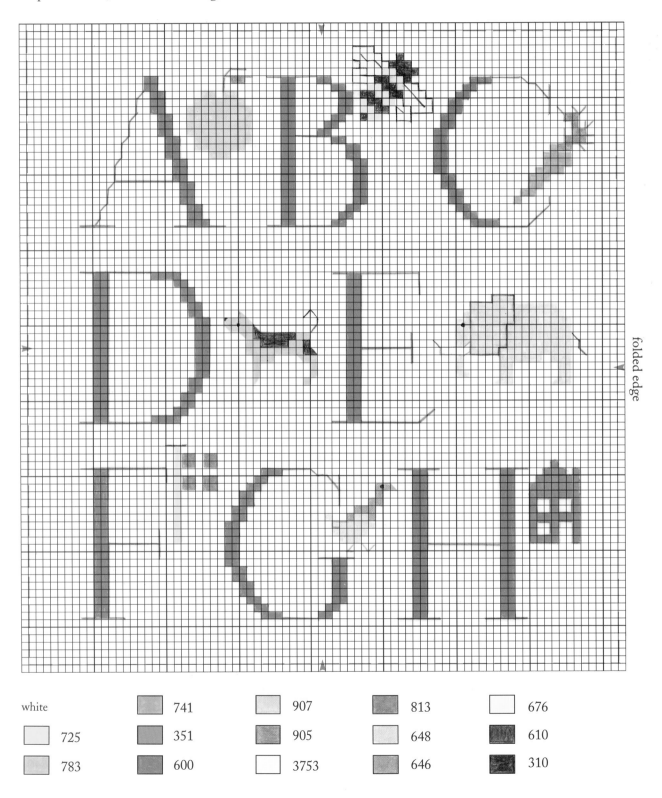

folded edge

white		741		907		813		676
	725		351		905		648		610
	783		600		3753		646		310

Ice cream and inner stripes of jug are stitched in white

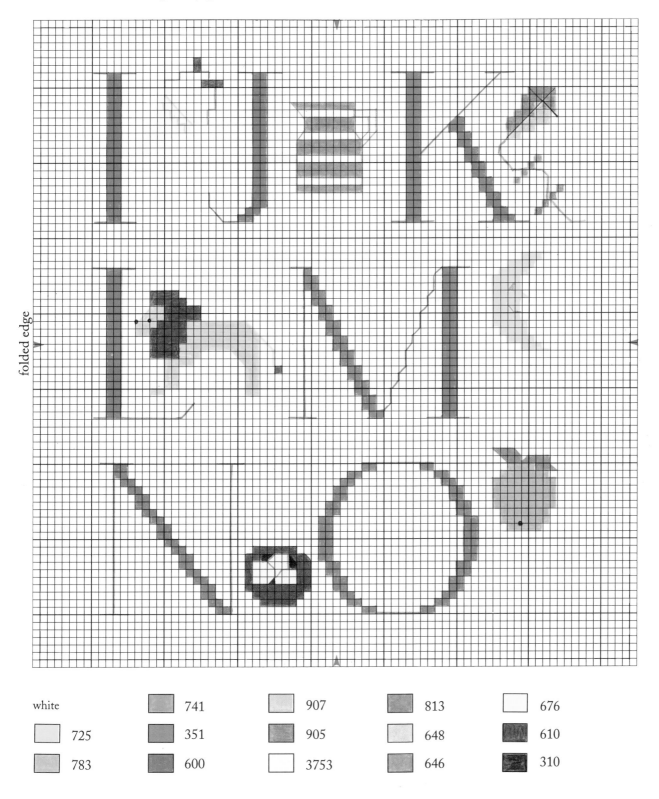

white		741		907		813		676
	725		351		905		648		610
	783		600		3753		646		310

folded edge

Wheels of truck are stitched in white

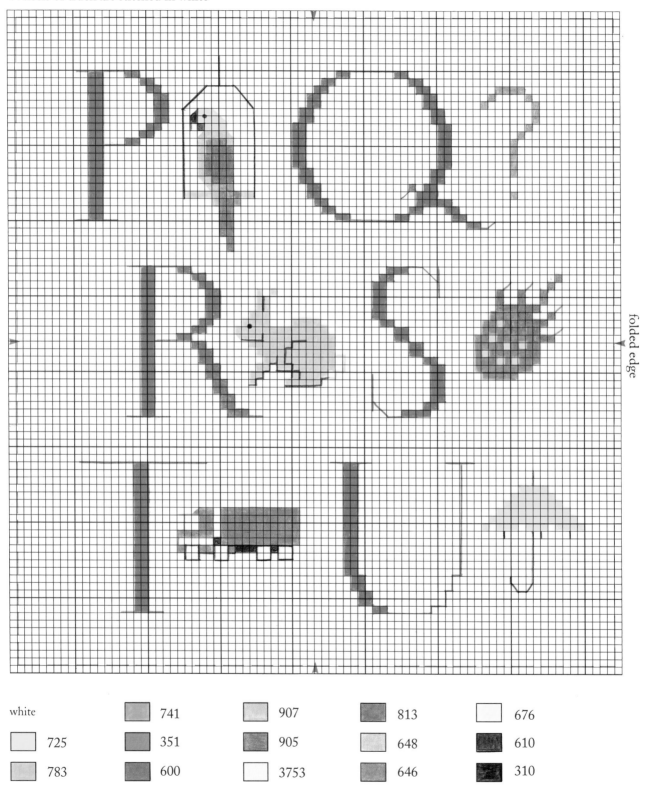

folded edge

white		741		907		813		676
	725		351		905		648		610
	783		600		3753		646		310

Watch face, yacht sail and zebras' stripes are stitched in white

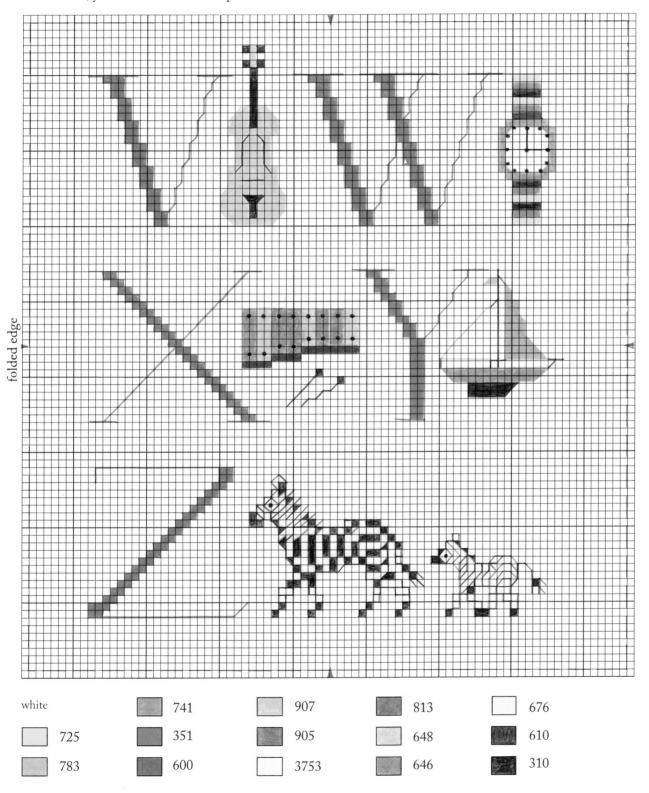

folded edge

white	741	907	813	676
725	351	905	648	610
783	600	3753	646	310

DOLL'S CRADLE QUILT AND PILLOW

In designing this tiny quilt and pillow cover, I'm reminded of just how much I adored my own doll's cradle—which I still have—and what joy I felt when an aunt made a down comforter especially for it.

This quilt and pillow cover design is based on pieced patchwork where different printed and woven fabrics are stitched together in geometric patterns. In old patchwork, the best parts of discarded garments would have been included and sometimes the colors were faded, which is an element I have used in my cross-stitched version. The small heart-print patches around the diamond are also a mixture of lighter and darker pinks.

Golden slumbers kiss your eyes,
Smiles, pretty wanton, do not cry,
And I will sing a lullaby:
Rock them, rock them, lullaby.

A CRADLE SONG

Thomas Dekker (c. 1572 - 1632)

The finished quilt measures 23 cm (9 in) square and the pillow 11.5 cm × 7.5 cm (4½ in × 3 in).

⌐ MATERIALS

White evenweave fabric, 25 threads to
  2.5 cm (1 in): two pieces 28 cm
  (11 in) square for the quilt and two
  pieces 18 cm × 13 cm (7 in × 5 in)
  for the pillow
Tacking (basting) thread
Tapestry needle size 26
Embroidery hoop (optional)
DMC 6-strand embroidery floss:
  see the thread list below
25 cm (10 in) square medium-weight
  synthetic wadding (batting)
Matching sewing thread
Crewel needle size 5

⌐ THREAD LIST

727 pale yellow
742 bright yellow
3820 deep yellow
775 pale blue
3755 blue
798 deep blue
3713 pale pink
760 pink
472 lime green
703 green
992 viridian green
731 olive green

⌐ THE EMBROIDERY

Both the quilt and the pillow are worked in the same way. On one of the two pieces of evenweave, mark the center both ways with tacking (basting) stitches. Work the embroidery in a hoop (see page 149) or in the hand, as preferred.

Following the color key and the appropriate chart, where each square represents one cross stitch worked over two threads of fabric, begin the embroidery in the middle using two strands of thread in the needle throughout. Complete the embroidery and carefully steam press on the wrong side.

⌐ MAKING THE QUILT

Trim the embroidery leaving 12 mm (½ in) seam allowances all around. Place it face down, center the wadding (batting) on top and then lay the backing fabric (the second piece of evenweave) over the wadding, right

Stitched and quilted cradle quilt

side uppermost, carefully smoothing the layers in place. Pin and tack (baste) the layers together, stitching diagonally in both directions. Using a single strand of olive green 731, and following the stitch lines on the chart, quilt through all layers working outward from the middle. Score the quilting lines using a ruler and tapestry needle. Using deep blue 798, quilt around the inner square (see the chart).

⌐ FINISHING THE EDGES

Trim the wadding (batting) by 12 mm (½ in) all around. Turn under the seam allowances of the top and backing taking the top turning over the edge of the wadding (batting). Pin and tack (baste) around the edge and, using matching thread, slipstitch to secure. Then, give your quilt a traditional finish by quilting close to the edge with matching thread.

⌐ MAKING THE PILLOW

Trim the embroidery as for the quilt, pin wadding (batting) only behind the pillow top and, using a single strand of green 703, quilt around the diamond, as shown on the chart. Using deep blue 798, quilt along the inside of the border.

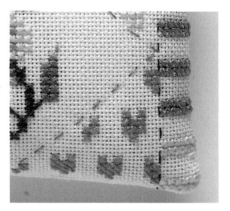

Stitched and quilted pillow

Place the back and front together, right sides facing, pin and stitch around close to the embroidery, leaving one short side open. Trim the seam allowances, cut across the corners and turn through to the right side. Lightly stuff with teased-out wadding (batting). Turn in the opening edges and slipstitch to close.

DOLL'S CRADLE QUILT AND PILLOW

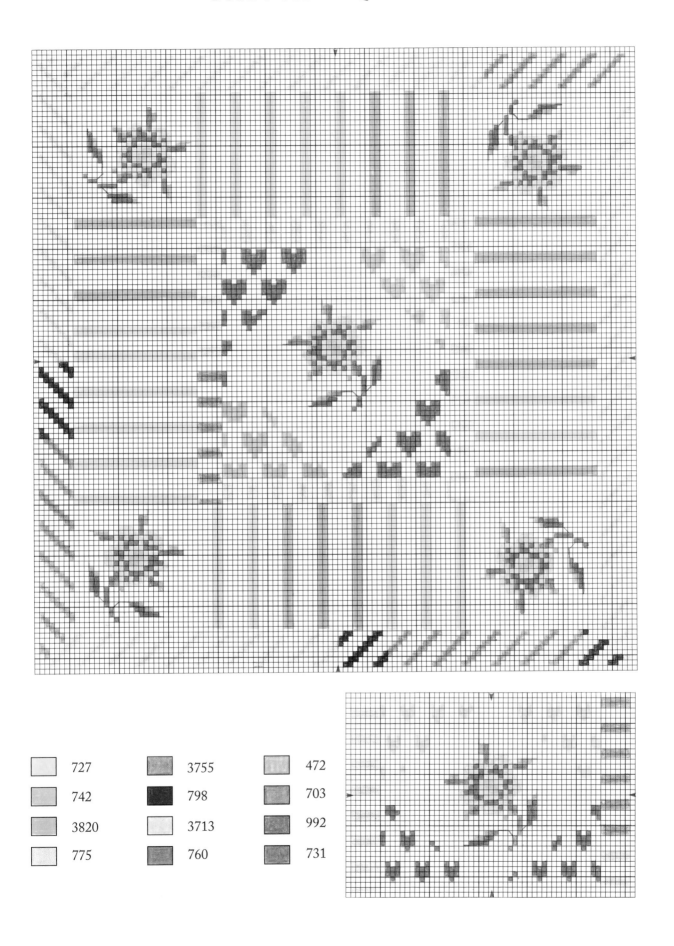

727	3755	472
742	798	703
3820	3713	992
775	760	731

CHILD'S PILLOW

Making a gift for a child is a pleasure in itself, but the greatest reward is in giving it. A child's natural curiosity and delight make all the effort seem well worthwhile. This full-sized child's pillow was inspired by the paintings and drawings of my six-year-old granddaughter, whose lively and sunny disposition shines through her art so clearly.

I have designed the cover in a patchwork style so that, should you decide to leave out any of the four motifs, there is still overall interest created by the different edge stitches and patches of contrasting fabrics. The large fabric buttons (handmade) are part of the design and should not be replaced with others made from hard materials such as pearl or plastic.

~

Child of the pure unclouded brow
And dreaming eyes of wonder!

THROUGH THE LOOKING-GLASS AND WHAT ALICE FOUND THERE

Lewis Carroll (1832-98)

The finished pillow measures
65 cm × 43 cm (25½ in × 17 in).

☞ MATERIALS

76 cm × 50 cm (30 in × 20 in) of white
  evenweave cotton, 27 threads to
  2.5 cm (1 in)
Tacking (basting) thread
Embroidery hoop (optional)
DMC 6-strand embroidery floss:
  see the thread lists below
Tapestry needle size 26
25 cm × 20 cm (10 in × 8 in) of blue
  and white checked gingham
20 cm × 15 cm (8 in × 6 in) of blue and
  white candy striped cotton fabric
46 cm × 15 cm (18 in × 6 in) of pink
  and white horizontal striped cotton
  fabric
Matching sewing threads
Crewel needle size 6
76 cm × 46 cm (30 in × 18 in) of white
  cotton fabric for the pillow back
5 cm × 2.5 cm (2 in × 1 in) of
  interfacing for the buttons

☞ THREAD LISTS

House and garden

445   pale yellow
783   burnt orange
828   turquoise
341   blue
471   green
992   viridian green
3052 sap green
3712 deep salmon pink
606   red
209   mauve
610   brown

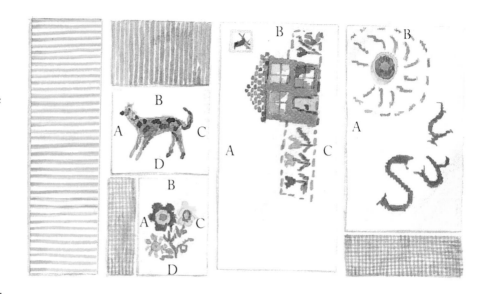

Piecing diagram

Dog

676   buff
3820 yellow
610   brown

Flower

445   pale yellow
783   burnt orange
471   green
992   viridian green
3689 pink
606   red
209   mauve
341   blue

Sun

445   pale yellow
834   pale olive
972   bright yellow
783   burnt orange
606   red
209   mauve

☞ THE EMBROIDERY

Following the measurement diagram
to the right, cut out the evenweave
fabric to size. On each piece of fabric
mark the center both ways with
tacking (basting) stitches. Work the
embroidery in a hoop (see page 149),
or in the hand, as preferred.

Following the appropriate chart,
where each square is equal to one
stitch worked over two threads—with
the exception of the house, where
larger stitches are worked over four
threads on the housefront and the
door—complete the embroidery using
two strands of thread in the needle.
Work the backstitch details on top.
Steam press on the wrong side and
retain the tacking (basting) stitches.

☞ MAKING THE PILLOW COVER

In order to give the pillow cover its
random patchwork effect, trim the
embroidered 'patches' as follows (all
measurements include 12 mm [½ in]

seam allowances throughout, and the letters match those on the piecing diagram, left):

House On edges A and B trim 2.5 cm (1 in), on edge C, 12 mm (½ in)

Dog On edges A and C trim 2.5 cm (1 in), on edges B and D, 4 cm (1½ in).

Flower On edges A, B and C trim 2.5 cm (1 in), on edge D, 12 mm (½ in)

Sun On edge A trim 2.5 cm (1 in), on edge B, 4 cm (1½ in)

From the blue checked fabric, cut two rectangles measuring 24 cm × 11.5 cm (9½ in × 4½ in) and 20 cm × 8.5 cm (8 in × 3¼ in), 12 mm (½ in) seams are included. From the blue and white striped fabric, cut a rectangle measuring 20 cm × 14 cm (8 in × 5½ in).

Following the piecing diagram, machine stitch the gingham and the flower patch together along side A with right sides facing. Press seam open. Then, join the remaining patches together in the same way, stitching the horizontal seams first to make four separate blocks. Join these together along the vertical seams to complete the front piecing. Press all seams open.

Using three strands of red 606, work blanket stitch (see page 152) around the sun patch. Continue with the same color along the gingham seam with running stitches (see page 152). Repeat this on the seam of the blue and white striped fabric. Using green 471, embroider herringbone stitch (see page 152) around edges B, C and D of the dog patch. Using pinks 3689 and 3712, work blanket

stitch along the edges of the flower that are marked A and C.

On the white cotton fabric (the pillow backing), make a double turning along one short edge, turning under 2.5 cm (1 in) and then 7.5 cm (3 in). Machine stitch across.

Place the front and back sections with right sides together, pin and stitch around three sides, leaving the pink and white striped fabric side open and extending beyond the opening edge. Trim the corners. Make a single turning on the side edges of the pink and white fabric, and make a 2.5 cm (1 in) turning on the long edge. Turn to the wrong side, pin and tack (baste). Machine stitch from the right side.

✎ BUTTONS AND BUTTONHOLES
On the front section, make two buttonholes 15.5 cm (6 in) apart. Unpick the seam for about 2.5 cm (1 in) and overcast the edges with red and blue threads. For the buttons, cut out two 5 cm (2 in) diameter circles from the white cotton fabric and two 2.5 cm (1 in) diameter circles from the interfacing. Make a tiny hem and, using double thread, run small stitches around the edge. Tightly pull up the thread and overcast the gathers in the center. Flatten the shape into a circle and stitch to the back opening hem to correspond with the buttonholes. Attach with large cross stitches in red and blue threads.

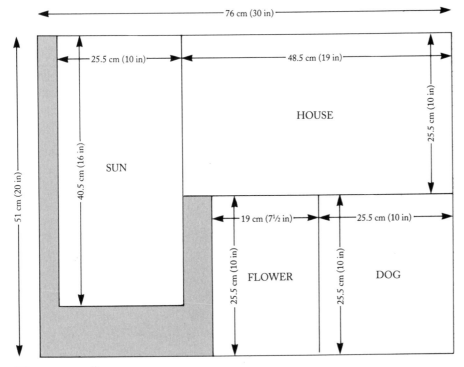

Measurement diagram

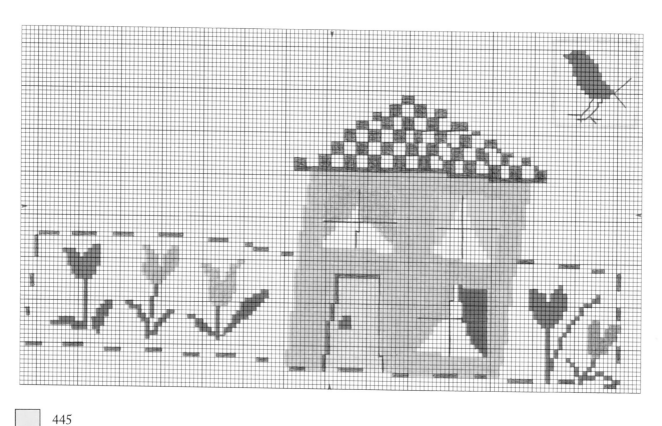

445
783
828
341
471
992
3052
3712
606
209
610

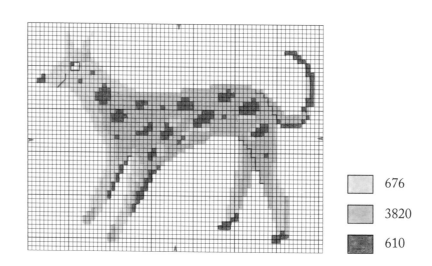

676
3820
610

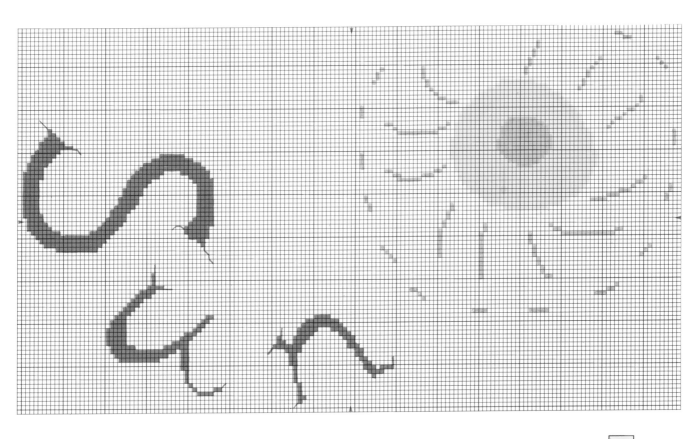

	445
	834
	972
	783
	606
	209

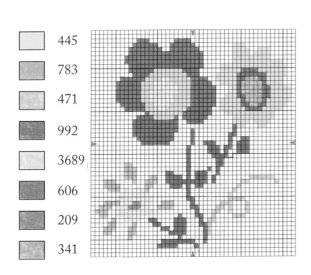

	445
	783
	471
	992
	3689
	606
	209
	341

SPECIAL CELEBRATIONS

~

GREETING CARD PICTURE

When I came to design this picture, I was attracted to the idea of sending a combined present and greeting card. The overall design was inspired by a cloister window overlooking a garden scene of great tranquility, which had a simple rose-covered arch set against a plain blue sky.

On the reverse side of the picture I've hidden a pocket in which a separate handmade greetings card is placed. This is made from stiff paper and edged with lace, although for some recipients you may wish to leave out the lace.

The picture has a fine twisted cord for hanging. Such a picture can often be made quite economically from small remnants which you may already have in your sewing bag.

~

*The manner of giving is
worth more than the gift.*

LE MENTEUR
Pierre Corneille (1606-84)

The finished greeting card picture measures 21.5 cm × 16.5 cm (8½ in × 6½ in).

☞ MATERIALS
20.5 cm (8 in) square of blue Aida, 14 threads to 2.5 cm (1 in)
20 cm × 23 cm (8 in × 9 in) of pale green evenweave, 14 threads to 2.5 cm (1 in)
Tacking (basting) thread
Tapestry needle size 24
DMC 6-strand embroidery floss: see the thread list to the right
Tracing paper
20 cm × 23 cm (8 in × 9 in) of interfacing
40 cm (16 in) of dusty pink satin ribbon, 6 mm (¼ in) wide
20 cm × 13 cm (8 in × 5 in) of blue and white small check or striped cotton lawn
Floral bias binding, 2.5 cm (1 in) wide
Matching sewing threads
Two pieces of stiff paper 7.5 cm × 10 cm (3 in × 4 in)
Spray adhesive
50 cm (20 in) of lace trim, 2.5 cm (1 in) wide

Detail of made-up card

☞ THREAD LIST
Top Section

472	lime green
3817	viridian green
470	sap green
605	pale pink
603	pink
601	deep pink

Lower Section

605	pale pink
603	pink
601	deep pink
3078	pale yellow
725	yellow
470	green

☞ THE EMBROIDERY
On the blue fabric mark the vertical center and baseline (positioned 2 cm [¾ in] in from the bottom edge), with tacking (basting) stitches. Work the embroidery in a hoop (see page 149) or in the hand, as preferred. Following the color key and the chart, where each square represents one cross stitch worked over one intersection of fabric, begin the embroidery in the middle. Working outward from the center, complete the cross stitching using two strands of thread in the needle. Add the backstitch details last of all. Lightly steam press on the wrong side. From the green fabric, cut off 9 cm (3½ in) for the lower section. Mark the center both ways and complete the embroidery as before.

☞ MAKING THE PICTURE
Trace the outline of the picture given opposite. Turn the tracing paper over,

and with the center line matching, trace off the second half in reverse and cut out. Using this as a pattern, cut out the interfacing to shape. Trim the edges of the green fabric evenly to measure 16.5 cm × 5cm (6½ in × 2 in). Trim the side edges of the blue fabric to 16.5 cm (6½ in) across and two thread intersections below the tacked (basted) baseline. Pin both fabrics in position on the interfacing with the

Ribbon-covered fabric seam

straight edges close together, and tack (baste) diagonally across the middle and around the edge. With the wrong side facing, cut around the blue fabric closely following the edge of the interfacing.

Cover the seam of the two fabrics with pink ribbon. Pin in place and hand stitch both edges using two strands of purple 3746 and running

GREETING CARD PICTURE

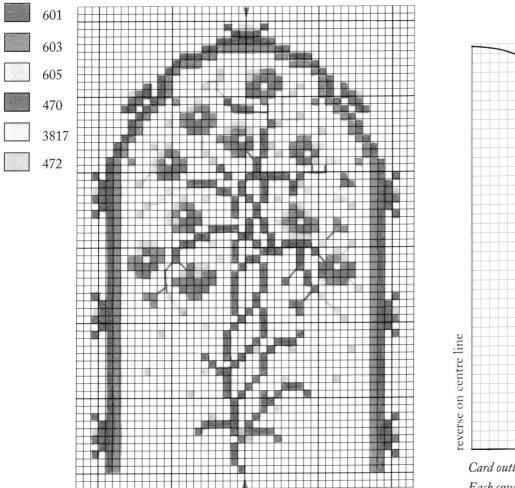

601	
603	
605	
470	
3817	
472	

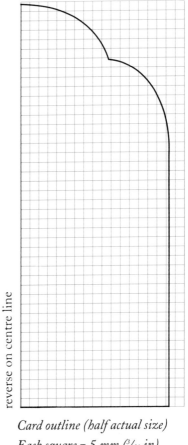

reverse on centre line

Card outline (half actual size)
Each square = 5 mm (³⁄₁₆ in)

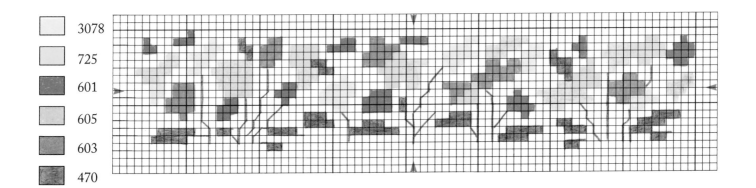

3078	
725	
601	
605	
603	
470	

stitches. On the remaining green fabric make a single narrow hem along one long edge, tack (baste) and press. Cover the raw edge with the pink ribbon and hand stitch both edges as before.

Using the paper pattern, cut out the blue and white lawn to shape. With wrong sides together, position the blue and white fabric on the back of the interfacing towards the top, and tack (baste) to hold. To make the pocket, pin the green fabric below with the right side facing and with the finished edge overlapping the blue and white fabric. Tack (baste) all the way around the edge to keep in place.

Working from the wrong side, cover the edge with bias binding. Turn under the raw edge before overlapping the starting point (see page 154). Fold the binding to the front and machine stitch through all layers.

Using two strands of lime green 472, make a twisted cord 45 cm (18 in) long (see page 154). Knot the ends to secure and fray the threads into tassels. Fold the cord in half and overcast the loop to the middle of the top edge. Knot the cords together to form a hanging loop.

☞ MAKING THE CARD
On one piece of paper, rule guidelines in pencil and write your greeting. On the second piece of paper spray adhesive on one side. Place the lace around the edge and press to hold. Spray the underside of the greeting and press the two pieces carefully together.

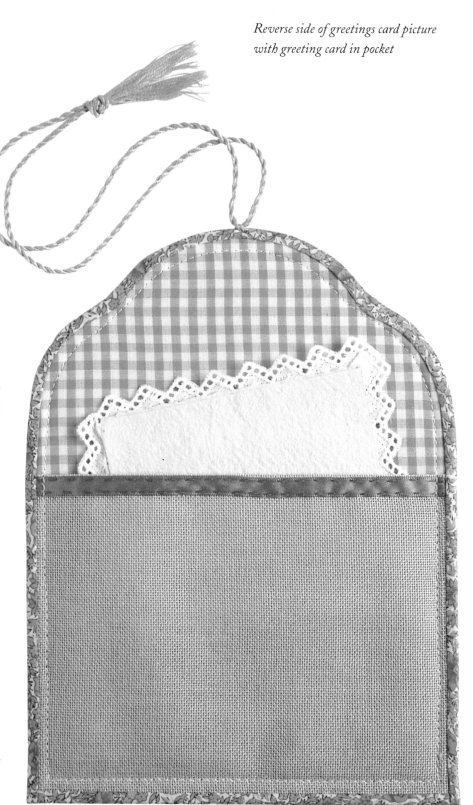

Reverse side of greetings card picture with greeting card in pocket

GREETING CARD SACHET

The custom of exchanging greeting cards between family and friends originated with the Victorians, who produced beautifully color-printed cards and some of the most exquisite confections in paper lace.

Flower motifs in particular were popular because of the then-current interest in the deeper meanings they conveyed: for example, forget-me-nots for true love, lily of the valley for the return of happiness, roses for love, and the pansy for thoughts and so on.

My parents had a collection of these cards, which I remember well, and the floral cards were the main inspiration for the sachet, in which an embroidered or handwritten card can be sent.

~

*Liberality lies less in giving
than in the timeliness of the gift.*

LES CARACTERES

Jean de la Bruyère (1645-96)

The finished sachet is
22 cm × 15.5 cm (8½ in × 6 in).

☞ MATERIALS

36 cm (14 in) square of antique white
   linen, 32 threads to 2.5 cm (1 in)
Tacking (basting) thread
Tapestry needle size 26
Embroidery hoop (optional)
DMC 6-strand embroidery floss:
   see the thread list below
28 cm (11 in) square of white muslin
   for interlining
28 cm (11 in) square of pale apricot
   cotton lawn for the lining
50 cm × 6.5 cm (20 in × 2½ in) of deep
   apricot cotton lawn for the frill
60 cm (24 in) of deep apricot satin
   ribbon, 3 mm (⅛ in) wide
Matching sewing threads
15.5 cm × 13 cm (6 in × 5 in) of off-
   white evenweave fabric, 16 threads
   to 2.5 cm (1 in) for the embroidered
   greeting card
Spray adhesive
10 cm × 13 cm (4 in × 5 in) of apricot
   cartridge paper
15.5 cm × 13 cm (6 in × 5 in) of off-
   white handmade paper for the
   handwritten greeting card

☞ THREAD LIST

472 lime green
743 yellow
761 pink
3712 deep salmon pink
828 pale blue
519 blue
471 grass green
989 green
590 sap green

☞ THE EMBROIDERY

Fold the linen in half both ways and
lightly crease. Measuring outward
from the middle, mark a 25 cm
(10 in) square with tacking (basting)
stitches. Into the bottom right-hand
corner work the forget-me-not motif
matching the tacked (basted) line to
the dotted line on the chart. Work
the embroidery in a hoop
(see page 149) or in the hand, as
preferred.

Detail of made-up sachet

Follow the color key and the chart on
page 106, where each square is equal
to one stitch worked over two fabric
threads. Begin the embroidery at the
outer edge and work toward the
center of the fabric using two strands
in the needle. Complete the cross
stitching and add the backstitching
last. On fairly open fabrics do not
strand your embroidery threads across
the back, otherwise they will be seen
from the right side. Lightly press on
the wrong side, and retain the tacking
(basting) stitches.

☞ MAKING THE SACHET

Trim the linen outside the tacked
(basted) line, adding a 12 mm (½ in)
seam allowance all around. On the
opposite corner from the embroidery,
trim away the corner to a depth of
3 cm (1¼ in) (see assembling
diagram). Trim the muslin and lining
fabric to match, then place the muslin
on the wrong side of the linen and pin
to hold. Trim across the corners and
fold over the seam allowance onto the
muslin, and tack (baste) around the
edge. Place the lining and the linen
wrong sides together, pin and tack
(baste) diagonally across in both
directions. Following the
measurement diagram , and using a
single strand of pink 761, quilt
random wavy lines across the surface
(about 2.5 cm [1 in] apart), omitting
them from the sachet flap. Working
freehand, score the linen with the
point of a needle as a guideline for
quilting.

   To make the frill, fold the deep
apricot fabric lengthwise in half, right
sides facing, and stitch the two short
ends. Trim the corners, turn through
and press. Run two rows of gathering
stitches inside the raw edge. Pull up
the gathers so that the frill fits around
the flap. Pin and tack (baste) it to the
inside edge of the sachet flap together
with one half of the ribbon, stitched
to the point of the flap. Fold under the
seam allowance of the lining, pin both
layers together and tack (baste)
around the edge. Secure the edge with
running stitches using a single strand
of pink 761. Following the diagram,
work a line of running stitches also in

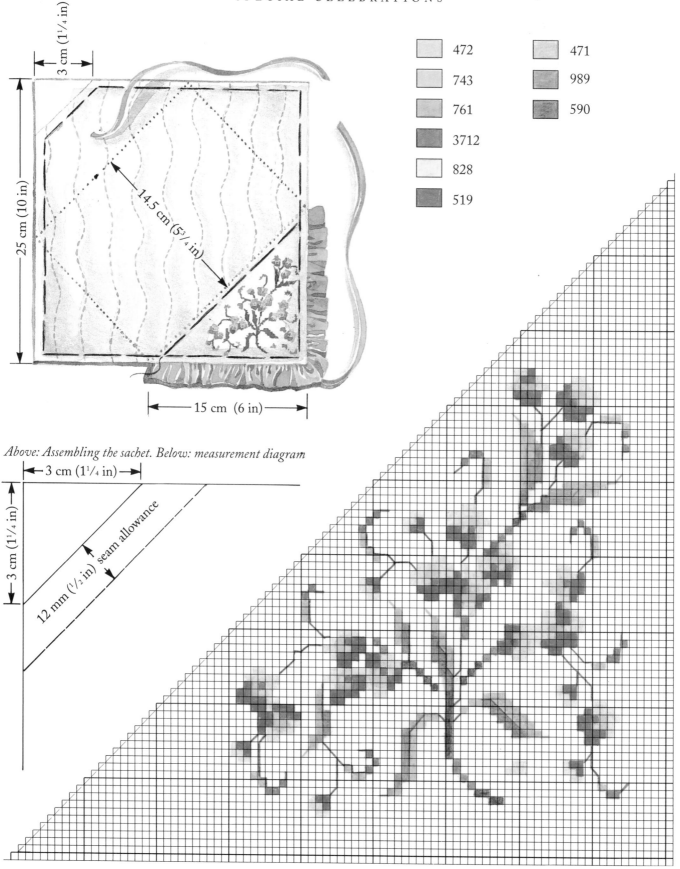

3 cm (1¹/₄ in)

25 cm (10 in)

14.5 cm (5³/₄ in)

15 cm (6 in)

472   471
743   989
761   590
3712
828
519

Above: Assembling the sachet. Below: measurement diagram

3 cm (1¹/₄ in)

3 cm (1¹/₄ in)

12 mm (¹/₂ in) seam allowance

GREETING CARD SACHET

3712
828
519
590

pink 761 across the fold of the flap.

With the right side out, fold the points of the sachet towards the center and neatly press the folds. Using two strands of pink 761, join the seams with single insertion stitch (see page 151).

Apply the second half of the ribbon to the front of the sachet to correspond with the ribbon on the flap. Cut the end of the ribbon to a point and prod it through the linen threads for 12 mm (½ in). Using matching thread, overstitch the ribbon end to the lining to finish.

◠ THE EMBROIDERED CARD
Follow the color key and chart, where each square represents one cross stitch and one backstitch, and outline the greeting using deep salmon pink 3712. Then complete the greeting in backstitch and the flowers in cross stitch. Lightly press on the wrong side. Using spray adhesive, coat one side of the cartridge paper and apply it centrally to the wrong side of the embroidery. Press firmly. To

finish the edge of the card, fray the fabric around the edges, up to the cartridge paper.

◠ THE PAPER CARD
Lightly rule fine guidelines with a ruler and pencil following the example given, and handwrite the greeting, substituting your particular names. Then, using colored thread of your choice, overcast the edges, knotting the ends to finish.

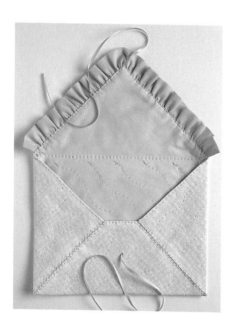

Seams joined with insertion stitch

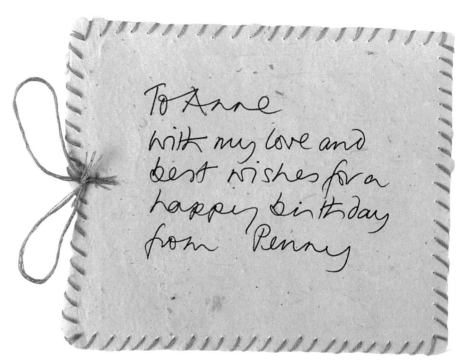

O Lord! thou knowest how busy I must be this day:
if I forget thee, do not thou forget me.

PRAYER BEFORE THE BATTLE OF EDGEHILL (SIR PHILIP WARWICK, MEMOIRES, 1701)

Sir Jacob Astley (1579-1652)

NEW BABY GREETING CARD

Having recently made a similar card for a friend's granddaughter, it looked so pretty and was received with such enthusiasm, I thought it should be included here. My idea was to design a small picture on a pink rosebud background, as though it were hung on a nursery wall. (For a boy, you might decide to change the pink for cornflower blue or deep yellow.)

If you would like to add second names or have double numerals to contend with, alter the design by extending the two sides of the miniature picture frame evenly to fit the extra numbers required, and put your baby's first name on the same line as baby. This would leave the bottom space for a second name and a longer date.

~

Where did you come from, baby dear?
Out of the everywhere into here.

AT THE BACK OF THE NORTH WIND

George MacDonald (1824-1905)

SPECIAL CELEBRATIONS

The finished greeting card measures 20 cm × 14 cm (8 in × 5½ in) with a cut-out measuring 14 cm × 9.5 cm (5½ × in 3¼ in).

☞ MATERIALS

Graph paper (optional)

26 cm × 20 cm (10 in × 8 in) of white Aida fabric, 18 threads to 2.5 cm (1 in)

Tacking (basting) thread

Tapestry needle size 26

Embroidery hoop (optional)

DMC 6-strand embroidery floss: see the thread list below

64 cm (25 in) pale pink and green satin ribbon, 3 mm (⅛ in) wide

Self-adhesive card mount with landscape, rectangular cut-out (see page 157 for suppliers)

☞ THREAD LIST

3354 pink

3731 deep pink

471 green

Care is heavy, therefore sleep you;
You are care, and care must keep you.
Sleep, pretty wanton, do not cry,
And I will sing a lullaby:
Rock them, rock them, lullaby.

A CRADLE SONG

Thomas Dekker (*c.* 1572 - 1632)

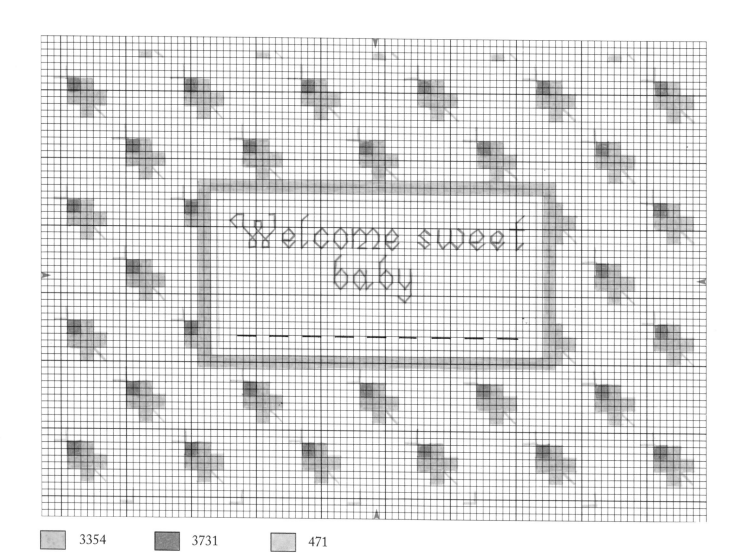

| ■ 3354 | ■ 3731 | □ 471 |

☞ CHART YOUR OWN NAME
AND DATE

Referring to the alphabet and numerals given on page 142, draw your details in the space provided on the chart in pencil.

If you need to extend the sides of the rectangle as mentioned earlier, then chart your names and longer date on the graph paper, centering them as shown in the diagram at right.

☞ THE EMBROIDERY

Mark the center of your fabric both ways with tacking (basting) stitches. Work the embroidery in a hoop (see page 149) or in the hand, as preferred. Following the color key and chart on page 110, where each

Detail of made-up card

square is equal to one cross stitch worked over one intersection of fabric, begin the cross stitching in the middle. Using two strands of thread in the needle, complete the motto and

Varying the lettering on the card

frame working outward from the center. Then embroider the rosebud background, stitching each bud separately–without stranding threads across the back of the fabric. Work the backstitch details at the same time as the leaves.

Lightly steam press the finished embroidery on the wrong side and retain the tacking (basting) stitches.

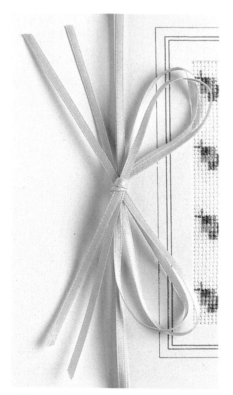

Ribbons tied around card

☞ ASSEMBLING THE CARD

Open out the self-adhesive card mount and place the embroidery centrally over the cut-out area, using the tacking (basting) as a guide. Trim the fabric 12 mm (½ in) bigger all around than the mounted area on the card. Remove the tacking (basting) and reposition the embroidery. Fold over the left-hand section and press firmly to secure. Tie the two ribbons around the card to finish in a bow.

☞ ADAPTING THE BASIC
GREETING CARD

The most important consideration when designing a greeting card for a new baby is to have enough space to spell out the first name(s) and the birth date.

Should your baby have two short names, you could delete 'babe'; and if the first name is longer, then delete 'sweet babe'. With a traditional border worked in cream and gold thread and a generous scattering of gold star sequins, this specially-made card could later be framed under glass as a keepsake for the new baby.

The finished greeting card measures 20 cm × 14 cm (8 in × 5½ in)

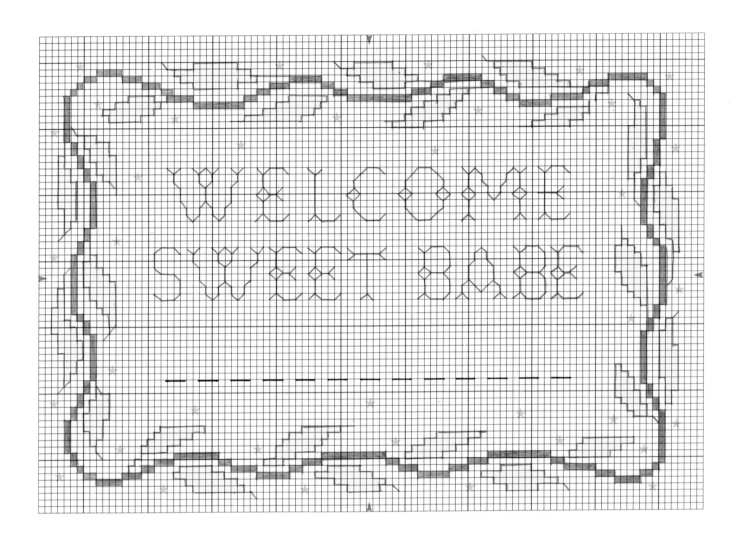

Graph paper (optional)
26 cm × 20 cm (10 in × 8 in) of white
  Aida fabric, 18 threads to 2.5 cm (1 in)
Tacking (basting) thread
Tapestry needle size 26
Embroidery hoop (optional)
DMC 6-strand embroidery floss:
  see the thread list to the right
64 cm (25 in) gold or white satin
  ribbon, 6 mm (¼ in) wide
Gold star-shaped sequins
Self-adhesive card mount with
  landscape, rectangular cut-out

☞ THREAD LIST

677   cream
      light gold thread

☞ MAKING THE GREETING
CARD

Following the basic instructions and
the alphabet on page 142, chart your
own name(s) and birth date on graph
paper or in the space provided on the
chart given. Similarly, embroider the
border design using two strands of
cream 677 and three strands of gold
thread in the needle. Backstitch the

	677
▨	light gold thread
✦	gold sequins

lettering using four strands of thread.
Following the chart, stitch the sequins
in position (see page 153). Assemble
the completed embroidery in the card
mount as previously instructed.

NEEDLEBOOK

My interest in embroidery items began when, as a very small child, I was allowed to tidy my mother's sewing box. Inside were beautiful things such as tiny mother-of-pearl cotton reels, thread winders, bodkin cases, pincushions, needlecases, and many more intriguing implements. In fact, the very first project I ever made as a child was a simple needlebook made from dark blue cotton – stitched with my mother's guidance. It had several leaves of flannel to hold the needles, and on the front cover I embroidered 'Needles' in red and then tied it around the spine with a bright red tasseled cord I'd kept from a Christmas card. Making it gave me enormous pleasure. On the back of your needlebook, you may like to work the numerals, as shown in the chart, or simply add your initials.

~

Here files of pins extend their shining rows,
Puffs, powders, patches, bibles, billets-doux.

THE RAPE OF THE LOCK
Alexander Pope (c. 1786-1872)

The finished needlebook measures
6.5 cm × 9 cm (2½ in × 3½ in).

☞ MATERIALS

Two pieces 23 cm × 15 cm (9 in × 6 in)
of natural colored linen,
25 threads to 2.5 cm (1 in)
Tacking (basting) thread
Tapestry needle size 26
Embroidery hoop (optional)
DMC 6-strand embroidery floss:
see the thread list below
Four pieces of thin cardboard
measuring 6.5 cm × 9 cm
(2½ in × 3½ in)
Spray adhesive
Matching sewing threads
Crewel needle size 7
Two pieces of white flannel
13 cm × 7.5 cm (5 in × 3 in)
Pinking shears (optional)
70 cm (27 in) of red bead trim

☞ THREAD LIST

349   red
958   viridian green
783   yellow
341   blue
741   orange
704   bright green

☞ THE EMBROIDERY

Divide each piece of linen as follows:
cut a strip 15 cm × 4 cm (6 in × 1½ in)
for the spine and then cut the
remaining fabric in half to give two
pieces 15 cm × 9.5 cm (6 in × 3¾ in)
for the back and front. On one piece,
mark the center both ways with
tacking (basting) stitches and work
the embroidery in a hoop (see page
149) or in the hand, if preferred.

Following the color key and alphabet
chart on the next page, where one
square is equal to one cross stitch
worked over two fabric threads, begin
the embroidery in the middle using
two strands of thread in the needle.

On a second piece of fabric,
embroider the numerals design
(optional) in the same way. Lightly
press on the wrong side.

☞ MAKING THE NEEDLEBOOK

Place the front fabric section face
down. On one of the pieces of
cardboard, lightly spray around the
edge of one side and center it on top
of the fabric, adhesive side up. Trim
the fabric across the corners to within
3 mm (⅛ in). Fold the edges over,
keeping the fabric straight and the
design centered. Press to secure.

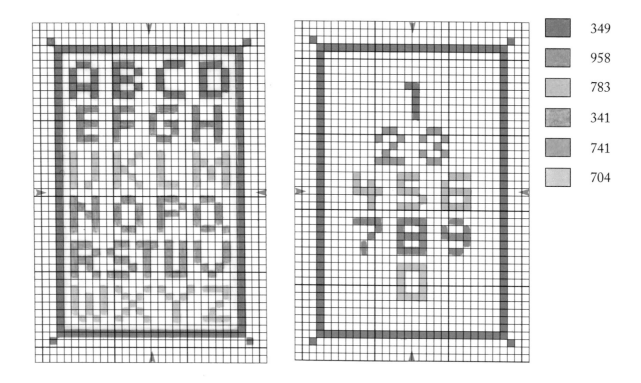

	349
	958
	783
	341
	741
	704

this for the back of the needlebook and on the two other pieces of cardboard, for the lining.

For the spine, make 3 cm (1¼ in) seam allowances on both short edges, fold them inward and press. With wrong sides facing, tack (baste) along the center to secure. With wrong sides uppermost, place the front and back of the needlebook side by side with a 12 mm (½ in) space between. Pin the spine centrally on top and, using matching thread, stitch through the spine catching the edge only of the covered boards. Do this on both sides of the spine to secure.

⌐ MARKER
Using two lengths of red 349 six-strand thread, make a twisted cord 20

(see page 154). Cover the knot with a 3 cm (1¼ in) tassel (see page 154).

⌐ LEAVES
Using pinking shears, trim around the edges of the flannel. Place both leaves together and stitch down the middle with running stitches.

⌐ ASSEMBLING THE PIECES
With the inside of the needlebook facing out, lay the marker inside the top edge of the back, close to the spine, and hold with a small piece of adhesive tape (see above right). On the wrong side of the cardboard lining pieces, spray adhesive and press each one firmly in place aligning the outside edges to the back and front

12 mm (½ in)

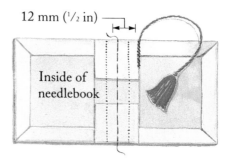

Assembling the pieces

Using matching thread, overcast the outside edges using tiny stitches. Apply bead trim to each side of the spine. Cover the outside edge of the needlebook with the bead trim, abutting the ends and oversewing firmly to secure. Finally, pin the leaves centrally inside the book and catch stitch to the inside fabric of the spine.

SEWING BAG WITH POCKETS

The original sewing bag, made from beautiful fine linen edged with red rickrack braid, was given to me by a great aunt when I was very young. I loved its size and was thrilled at how much I could carry in it. It took every sewing item I possessed including, no doubt, a small doll or two—and the pockets bulged with different colored sewing threads, old buttons, press studs, pins, needles and so on.

I remember taking it with me when I visited aunts and uncles just in case I had to 'get on with something' on my own. Times change, but there is always a need for a roomy sewing bag. It's one of the best organizers for keeping sewing things to hand—and it looks pretty as well.

~

Like a knitter drowsed,
Whose fingers play in skilled unmindfulness,
The Will has woven with an absent heed
Since life first was; and ever so will weave.

THE DYNASTS

Thomas Hardy (1840-1928)

SPECIAL CELEBRATIONS

The finished sewing bag measures
23 cm × 20 cm (9 in × 8 in).

⌒ MATERIALS
90 cm × 56 cm (36 in × 22 in) of white
    evenweave, 27 threads to
    2.5 cm (1 in)
Tacking (basting) thread
Tapestry needle size 26
Embroidery hoop (optional)
DMC 6-strand embroidery floss:
    see the thread list to the right
2.7 m (3 yd) of red rickrack braid
Matching sewing threads
1.85 m (2 yd) of white silk cord,
    3 mm (⅛ in) thick
Six old pearl buttons 1 cm (⅜ in)
    across
Large bodkin

⌒ THREAD LIST
3820 yellow
581   green
991   dark green
606   red
807   blue

⌒ THE EMBROIDERY
Press the evenweave fabric. Cut off
one length, 15.5 cm × 56 cm
(6 in × 22 in) for the sewing bag base,
and put to one side. Cut the
remaining fabric horizontally across to

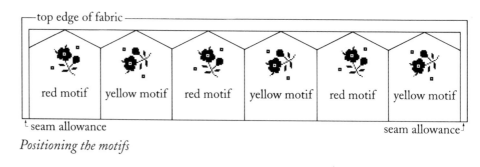

Positioning the motifs

▢	3820		
▢	581	■	606
■	991	▢	807

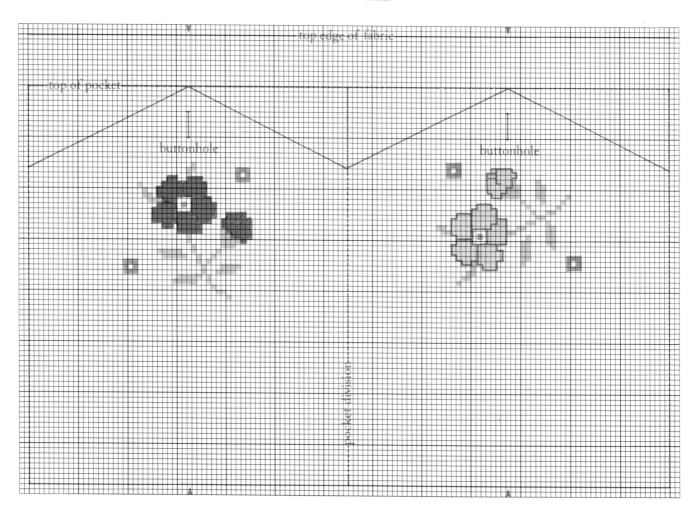

give one piece 76 cm × 20 cm
(30 in × 8 in) for the pockets and
another 76 cm × 30.5 cm
(30 in × 12 in) for the workbag.
Following the chart, mark the top of
the pockets and the pocket divisions
with tacking (basting) stitches and, as
shown in the diagram on page 118,
place each motif centrally on the
fabric in each pocket area.

Work the embroidery in a hoop (see
page 149) or in the hand, as preferred.
Following the color key and the chart
on page 118, where each square
represents one stitch worked over two
fabric threads, begin the embroidery
in the center of a motif, using two
strands of thread in the needle. Repeat
the two motifs as shown in the
diagram. Complete the cross stitching
and then outline the flowers using a
single strand of dark green 991.

☞ MAKING THE SEWING BAG

Trim the bottom edge of the
embroidered pocket section so that
the depth measures 18 cm (7 in) from
the top of the pockets. Trim the side
edges leaving 2 cm (¾ in) seam
allowances. With right sides facing,
pin and machine stitch the side seam
and press open.

Cut the sewing bag section vertically
in half and, with right sides facing, pin
and stitch the sides taking 2 cm (¾ in)
seams. Stitch to within 10 cm (4 in) of
the top edge. Press the seams open.
Make 1 cm (⅜ in) double hems on
both edges above the side seams, and
press. On the top edges turn 1 cm (⅜
in) to the wrong side and then 4 cm
(1½ in) once more; pin and machine

stitch across. Make the drawstring
channel by machine stitching a second
line 12 mm (½ in) above the first.

☞ APPLYING THE RICKRACK BRAID

Following the measurements given on
the chart, cut the pockets to shape
adding 6 mm (¼ in) seam allowances.
Cut six 17 cm (6½ in) lengths of
rickrack braid and tack (baste) them
over the previously tacked (basted)
lines dividing the pockets, leaving raw
edges at both ends. Snip into the
angles of the pockets and fold a single
6 mm (¼ in) hem to the right side on
each pocket top. Pin rickrack braid
over the turning, easing it so that the
points of the braid fall evenly on the
pocket points and into the angles.
Machine stitch along the braid with
red sewing thread.

☞ ASSEMBLING THE SEWING BAG

Place the sewing bag section inside
the pocket section, both with right
sides out and tack (baste) the bottom
edges together. Using red thread,
machine stitch the divisions of the
pockets, stitching through the
rickrack braid and all layers.

Run two rows of gathering threads
around the bottom edge just inside the
previously stitched seamline.

From the base section, cut out two
circles measuring 15.5 cm (6 in)
across. Tack (baste) the seamline
12 mm (½ in) from the edge on both
of the base pieces.

Pull up the gathers on the sewing
bag to fit the base. With right sides

facing, pin the gathers evenly to the
base. Tack (baste) and stitch on the
seamline. Notch the curved seam
allowance and press. Similarly, notch
and make a fold on the base lining.
Pin and hem in place the lining to
neaten the base.

Cut the cord in half and, using a
large bodkin, thread each length
through the channel starting from the
opposite sides. Finally, knot the
ends together.

☞ BUTTONS AND BUTTONHOLES

Cut the buttonholes as shown on the
chart and, using matching sewing
thread, buttonhole stitch around them

Buttons stitched in place

(see page 150). Lay the pocket section
flat and, with a pin placed centrally
through the buttonhole, mark the
positions of the buttons. Stitch them
in place using bright red thread.

FRIENDSHIP BRACELETS

The exchanging of fabric bracelets between friends is a charming custom. They are often made in the hand by finger-plaiting together differently colored yarns where the ends form a natural loop and tie.

I am not sure of their origin – I have a feeling it is Central America – but what I am sure about is that, once bracelets are exchanged, friendship is forever. I am told also that, for the friendship to endure, the bracelet should never be removed from the wrist or ankle, or wherever it may be worn. Alternatively, I received one not so long ago from a friend who chose to tie it around a small collection of candles. As friendship bracelets can so easily be made from the smallest scrap of fabric, and involve a minimum of cross stitching, even beginners to embroidery might be tempted to try their skill.

~

A faithful friend is the medicine of life.

ECCLESIASTES

Holy Bible Apocrypha

The finished bracelets measure
19 cm × 2 cm (7½ in × ¾ in), without
the ties.

☞ MATERIALS
25 cm × 6 cm (10 in × 2½ in) of red
  evenweave fabric, 27 threads to
  2.5 cm (1 in)
25 cm × 6 cm (10 in × 2½ in) of cream
  evenweave fabric, 28 threads to
  2.5 cm (1 in)
Tacking (basting) thread
Tapestry needle size 26
Embroidery hoop (optional)
DMC 6-strand embroidery floss:
  see the thread lists below
Small gold beads for the red bracelet
  (optional)
Crewel needle size 6
Matching sewing threads

☞ THREAD LIST (RED FABRIC)
725   yellow
501   dark green

☞ THREAD LIST (CREAM
FABRIC)
3821 yellow
3354 pink
3805 bright pink
503   mid-lovat green

☞ THE EMBROIDERY
Both bracelets are embroidered in the
same way. Mark the center of the
fabric both ways with tacking
(basting) stitches. Work the
embroidery in a hoop (see page 149)
or in the hand, as preferred. Small
amounts of fabric such as these are
easier to work in the hand.

  Following the appropriate color

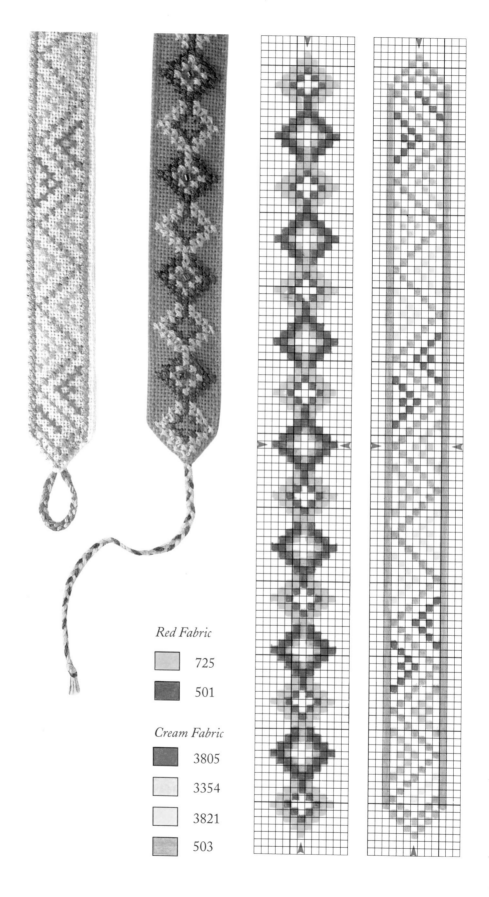

Red Fabric

725
501

Cream Fabric

3805
3354
3821
503

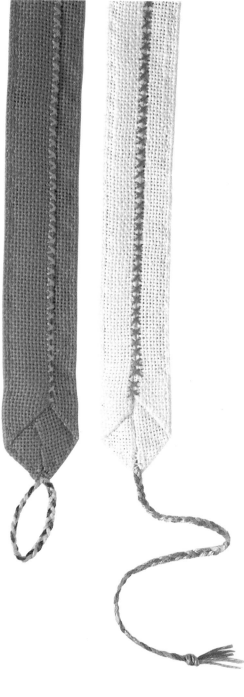

key and chart, where each square is equal to one stitch worked over two fabric threads, begin the cross stitching working outward from the center. Use two strands of thread in the needle throughout.

On the red bracelet, begin with the larger diamond in the middle using dark green 501. Complete the dark green cross stitching and add the yellow 725 diamonds in between. Sew a gold bead to the center of each large green diamond. Remove the tacking (basting) threads and lightly steam press on the wrong side.

On the cream bracelet, begin with the zigzag pattern, and then outline the bracelet using mid-lovat green 503. Fill in the triangular patterns to complete the embroidery.

⌒ MAKING THE BRACELETS
Trim the long edges of the fabric leaving 2 cm (¾ in) at each side of the embroidery (also 2 cm [¾ in] wide). Trim the two short sides to within 6 mm (¼ in) of the embroidery.

To make the pointed ends, follow

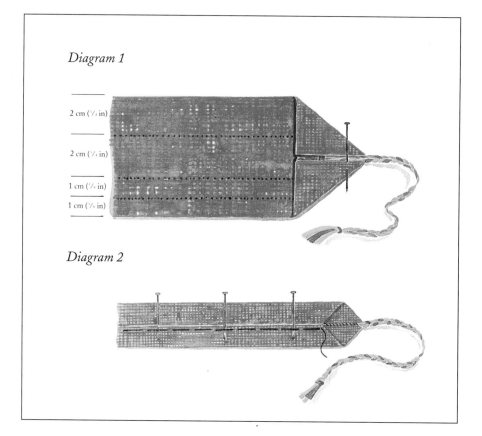

Diagram 1

2 cm (¾ in)

2 cm (¾ in)

1 cm (¼ in)

1 cm (¼ in)

Diagram 2

Cream fabric

the diagrams opposite and fold over the short end by 6 mm ($\frac{1}{4}$ in), then fold in each corner to the center and press flat. Repeat at the other end.

Make a loop and single tie by plaiting together three 15 cm (6 in) lengths of embroidery thread in mixed colors, using six strands each. Cut off 6.5 cm ($2\frac{1}{2}$ in), fold in half to make the loop and bind the cut ends securely. Bind the cut end of the remaining plait for the tie.

Insert the bound end of the loop under the folds at one pointed end and the tie under the other. Pin and slip hem the folds together, oversewing the plaits very securely at each point.

Fold one long edge over, taking a 2 cm ($\frac{3}{4}$ in) hem. Make a 1 cm ($\frac{3}{8}$ in) hem on the opposite side and fold it over the first hem. Pin, tack (baste) and decoratively cross stitch to hold along the center seam, stitching through the folded layers only. Using matching thread, top stitch the edges of the bracelet with running stitches. Remove the tacking (basting) and repeat for the second bracelet.

☞ ADAPTING THE BASIC
FRIENDSHIP BRACELETS
The combination of ground fabric colors and stitched motifs is endlessly variable. Take inspiration from the designs given or create your own patterns. Experiment by changing the color of the ground fabric, for example, to give totally different effects.

The longer designs given here are intended for a friendship choker and anklet but they can easily be made shorter for a bracelet, if preferred.

The finished choker measures 31 cm × 2 cm (12 in × $\frac{3}{4}$ in); the anklet, 20 cm × 2 cm (8 in × $\frac{3}{4}$ in).

☞ MATERIALS
For the choker:
38 cm × 6 cm (15 in × $2\frac{1}{2}$ in) of black
  evenweave fabric, 26 threads to
  2.5 cm (1 in)
For the anklet:
28 cm × 6 cm (11 in × $2\frac{1}{2}$ in) of white
  evenweave fabric, 26 threads to
  2.5 cm (1 in)
Tacking (basting) thread
Tapestry needle size 26
Embroidery hoop (optional)
DMC 6-strand embroidery floss:
  see the thread lists below

☞ THREAD LIST (CHOKER)
725   yellow   891   red
3811 turquoise

☞ THREAD LIST (ANKLET)
958   viridian green   917   red
792   blue

☞ MAKING THE CHOKER AND
ANKLET
Following the color key and the charts given to the right and the instructions for the basic bracelet, complete the embroidery. Make two plaited ties using three 20 cm (8 in) lengths of embroidery thread. Insert the ends into the folded ends of the choker or anklet and secure as for the bracelet. Tie in a bow to hold in place.

Black fabric

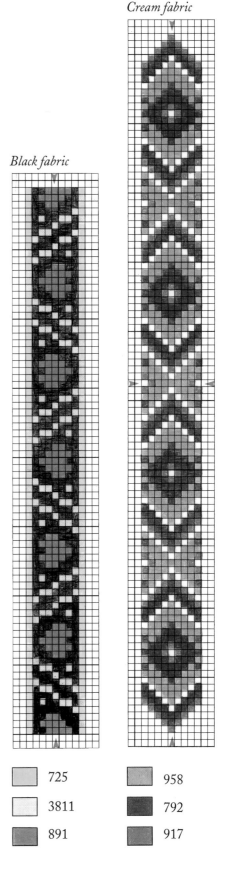

▢	725	▢	958
▢	3811	▢	792
▢	891	▢	917

PLAYING CARDS WALLET

Encapsulating all the flamboyance, color and style of fifteenth-century European court dress, traditional playing card designs make excellent graphic motifs, and can be interpreted in cross stitch to great effect.

This handy wallet has a deep pocket for holding a pack of cards, its edges are trimmed with a two-color twisted cord, and the top flap is secured with buttons and handmade loops. As an alternative fastening, you could use narrow ribbons in two colors tied in a pretty bow. The ribbons should be placed in the center of both opening edges and stitched within the seam.

~

A man's idea of a card game is war – cool, devastating and pitiless. A lady's idea of it is a combination of larcerny, embezzlement and burglary.

Finley Peter Dunne (1867-1936)

The finished wallet measures
9 cm × 11.5 cm × 2.5 cm
(3½ in × 4½ in × 1 in).

⌖ MATERIALS

32 cm × 20 cm (12½ in × 8 in) of
  antique white evenweave fabric,
  16 threads to 2.5 cm (1 in)
Tacking (basting) thread
Tapestry needle size 26
Embroidery hoop (optional)
DMC 6-strand embroidery floss:
  see the thread list below; allow one
  skein each of red 666 and blue 312
  for the twisted cord
Crewel needle size 7
32 cm × 20 cm (12½ in × 8 in) of off-
  white cotton lawn for the lining
32 cm × 20 cm (12½ in × 8 in) of
  lightweight interfacing
Matching sewing threads
Two small red buttons

⌖ THREAD LIST

725   pale yellow
3820 yellow
783   deep yellow
666   red
754   pink
      ecru
453   gray
310   black
312   blue

⌖ THE EMBROIDERY

On the evenweave fabric at the right-
hand side, mark a vertical line with
tacking (basting) stitches 5 cm (2 in)
in from the raw edge. Tack (baste)
the horizontal center line ready to
embroider the wallet flap. Working the
embroidery in a hoop (see page 149)

*It is very wonderful to see persons of the
best sense passing away a dozen hours together
in shuffling and dividing a pack of cards, with
no other conversation but what is made up of a
few game phrases, and no other ideas but those
of black and red spots ranged together in
different figures.*

Joseph Addison (1672-1719)

▢	725	▨	666	▨	453
▨	3820	▢	754	■	310
▨	783	□	ecru	▨	312

or in the hand, as preferred, begin the cross stitching in the middle. Following the color key and chart, where each square represents one stitch worked over one intersection of fabric, complete the design using two strands of thread in the needle. Work the backstitch details on top to finish. Lightly steam press on the wrong side, if needed.

☞ MAKING THE WALLET
Carefully following the measurement diagram below, mark the outline, as shown, on the wrong side with tacking (basting) stitches, counting the fabric threads to give an accurate finish. Following the same measurements, mark the outlines on the interfacing for the back, pocket and front flap and the four box sides using a pencil and ruler. Cut out just

I am sorry I have not learned to play at cards. It is very useful in life: it generates kindness and consolidates society.

TOUR TO THE HEBRIDES
Dr. Samuel Johnson (1709-84)

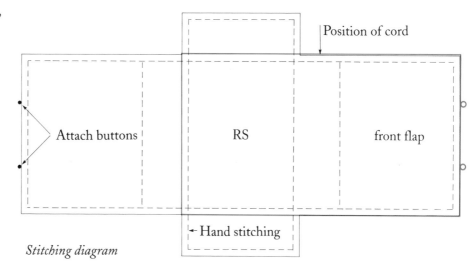

Stitching diagram

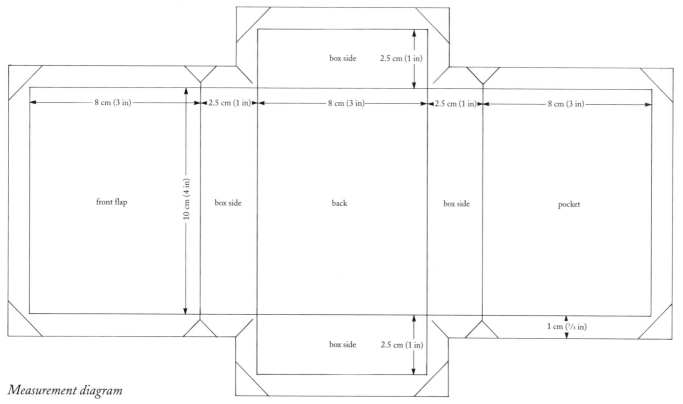

Measurement diagram

diagram. On the lining, fold under and tack (baste) in place.

With the wrong side of the evenweave facing, tack (baste) the pieces of interfacing in place. Fold over the hems, pin and tack (baste). With wrong sides facing, pin and tack (baste) the lining to the evenweave. Following the dotted lines on the stitching diagram (previous page), stitch around the wallet back and inside front using matching thread and small running stitches. Then, stitch around the outside edge with running stitches. Following the stitch diagram on page 151, slipstitch the corners of the box sides together.

Opened-out wallet

Using the red 666 and blue 312 six-strand embroidery threads, make a 56 cm (22 in) long twisted cord (see page 154), to fit the outside edges of the wallet. Again, following the stitch diagram and working from the right side, slipstitch the cord in place, twisting and tucking the two cut ends into the seam to neaten.

Attach two small red buttons to the opening edge (on the box side) and work button loops in red on the flap edge to correspond (see page 153).

Playing card wallet with red buttons and loops

inside the pencil line so that each section is slightly smaller than the evenweave. This will allow the sides to bend easily into a box shape.

Following the tacked (basted) outline and allowing 1 cm (³⁄₈ in) for

seams all around, cut out the evenweave. Using this as a pattern, pin the evenweave on the lining, straight grains matching, and cut out. Snip into the angles and trim across the outer corners as shown in the

INITIALED
BOOKMARK

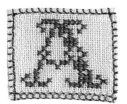

A single letter cross stitched on a small band of linen is the simplest way to make a bookmark. Some of the more decorative typefaces, such as this nineteenth-century German alphabet, lend themselves perfectly to cross stitch, where even a single letter becomes an interesting motif on its own.

The classic edging for a bookmark is hemstitching, whereby small groups of threads are bound tightly together and the remaining fabric fringed up to the stitching. This can be worked in matching sewing thread or in a contrasting color so that it becomes a design detail of the bookmark. Double hems are not recommended because of the bulk they would cause between the pages of a book.

~

A good book is the best of friends,
the same today and for ever.

PROVERBIAL PHILOSOPHY, 'OF READING'

Martin Farquhar Tupper (1810-89)

The finished bookmark measures 23 cm × 5 cm (9 in × 2 in).

☞ MATERIALS
25 cm × 10 cm (10 in × 4 in) of antique white linen, 28 threads to 2.5 cm (1 in)
Tacking (basting) thread
Tapestry needle size 26
DMC 6-strand embroidery floss: see the thread list below
Matching sewing thread

☞ THREAD LIST
3807   blue

Select your chosen initial from the alphabet on page 144 and mark the vertical center line with a pencil.

☞ THE EMBROIDERY
Mark the center of the linen both ways with tacking (basting) stitches. Following the chart, where each square represents one cross stitch worked over two fabric threads, count the squares from the middle and begin the embroidery with the initial using two strands of thread in the needle. Complete the initial.

Using a single strand of thread, work punch stitch around three edges of the bookmark . Work the stitch over three threads of fabric in both directions and on three sides of the stitch only, as shown in the diagram. Do not make a hem on the bottom edge and continue with punch stitch working through a single layer and working four sides to the stitch. Work a similar line of punch stitch under the initial.

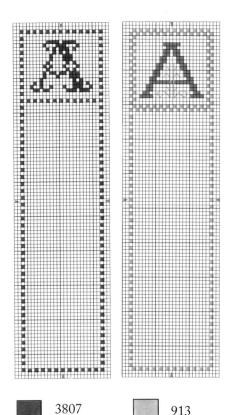

■	3807
□	913
■	350

Trim back the three turned edges close to the stitching. Fringe the bottom edge (see page 151), first cutting it to measure 3 cm (1¼ in). Remove the tacking (basting) threads and press on the wrong side to finish.

☞ ADAPTING THE BASIC INITIALED BOOKMARK
For a more colorful effect, embroider your chosen initial in two contrasting colors, cross stitching the letter and backstitching the floral line decoration. The small amount of fabric needed for a bookmark is ideal for using up leftovers which you may already have in your sewing bag in a variety of colors. The only point to remember is that the fabric gauge

should be 28 or 14 otherwise the initial will be larger or smaller than in the main instructions, and you will need to adjust accordingly. The edging can also be varied, in stitch and color, as described in the basic instructions.

The finished bookmark measures 23 cm × 5 cm (9 in × 2 in).

☞ MATERIALS
25 cm × 10 cm (10 in × 4 in) of cream evenweave fabric, 28 threads to 2.5 cm (1 in)
Tacking (basting) thread
Tapestry needle size 26
DMC 6-strand embroidery floss: see the thread list below
Matching sewing thread

☞ THREAD LIST
913   green   350   red

☞ MAKING THE BOOKMARK
Select your chosen initial from the alphabet on page 145. Then, following the basic instructions, complete the embroidery using either punch stitch or hem stitch to neaten the edges. Fringe the bottom edge to finish the bookmark.

Fringed bookmark

th century the language of the English royal
as French, and many people in the south o...
language to the other and mixing the two...
heard in Norman England; English peopl...
n this form that we know it today, altho...
sed in heraldry.

tremely useful in England, and a...
ish Dictionary reminds us how a...
s are in adapting old words to ne...
specialized: it ceased to be appli...
of shell. This narrower, more...
cations: it was the mollusc...
n baptism); a pilgrim's b...
op shell, and a collar h...
e the noun as a verb: t...   o
n scallops, or to bak...   ord
a less common w...   ne to
rs scallops. Such...   etween
ages, perhaps i...   emblance
ell' in English...   kle' and the
r, but there ar...   of the empty
osive shell, c...   oquille' meaning
it happens,...
plete object, expl...
rts to unravel its histor...   historic Germany to
related words from the fores...   if we did not also re-
. The story would not be compl...
has carried these words from Western Europe all over the
four hundred years has in fact been as dramatic as the tribal
Whereas in 1500 these words were almost entirely confined
w to be heard in one form or another in every continent; no
simplest of the SKAL words, has the largest currency of any
llop' is used wherever English is fully known, and 'escalope' is
peaking parts of the world, but wherever French cooking is

THE
LIVING SCALLO

W. J. Rees

$\mathcal{P}$INCUSHION

Some of the most innovative and decorative pincushions I have ever seen are those made in the nineteenth century by men serving in the army and navy. Sending pincushions to friends was a fashionable pastime then and many servicemen sent them back home as tokens of their love.

Such cushions were stuck with pins and colorful beads, and the design may have incorporated messages of devotion, to a mother, sister, or sweetheart, as well as regimental badges and buttons. They were impressively big and bold, and often had large ribbon bows and deep fringed edges overhung with decorative loops of beads.

I wanted to make a similar cushion that could be given as a present and which might be used for keeping jewelry safe.

I love thee for a heart that's kind –
Not for the knowledge in thy mind,

SWEET STAY-AT-HOME
W. H. Davies (1871-1940)

See a pin and pick it up,
All day the day you'll have good luck;
See a pin and let it lie,
You'll want a pin before you die.

PROVERB

The finished cushion measures
20 cm × 13 cm (8 in × 5 in), excluding
the handmade lace trim.

☞ MATERIALS
Graph paper
25 cm × 18 cm (10 in × 7 in) of white
   linen, 25 threads to 2.5 cm (1 in)
Tacking (basting) thread
Tapestry needle size 26
Embroidery hoop (optional)
DMC 6-strand embroidery floss:
   see the thread list to the right
1 × 20 g ball of white Coats Chain
   Mercer Crochet number 60 floss
1 pair of 2¾ mm (12) knitting needles
25 cm × 18 cm (10 in × 7 in) of white
   cotton damask
Loose synthetic wadding (batting)

1 m (39 in) of turquoise satin ribbon,
   6 mm (¼ in) wide
Matching sewing threads
Crewel needle size 7
Pins (optional)
Pale turquoise glass beads

☞ THREAD LIST
3822 yellow
3820 deep yellow
3819 lime green
959   green
3810 iridescent blue
963   pale pink
3716 pink
893   salmon pink
601   fuchsia
3687 rose pink
3811 pale turquoise
3766 turquoise

☞ ADDING YOUR OWN NAME
Using the alphabet given on page 143,
draw your chosen name on a piece of
graph paper, matching the grid to that
given in the book. For a longer name,
omit FOR and the middle motif and
center it in the remaining space.

☞ THE EMBROIDERY
Mark the center of your fabric both
ways with tacking (basting) stitches
and then stretch it in a (large) hoop
(see page 149), or work in the hand, as
preferred.

   Following the color key and the
chart, where each square represents
one stitch worked over two fabric
threads, begin the cross stitching in
the middle. Use two strands of thread

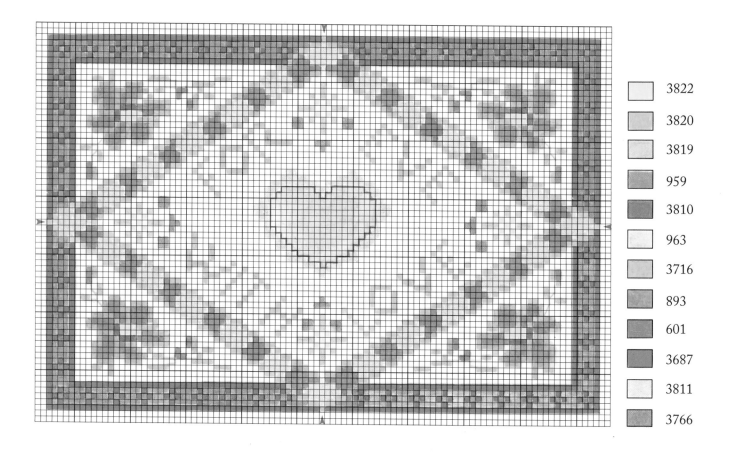

	3822
	3820
	3819
	959
	3810
	963
	3716
	893
	601
	3687
	3811
	3766

in the needle throughout, and complete the embroidery. Press lightly on the wrong side, if needed. Sew on the beads (see page 152) in the positions shown on the chart.

◐ LACE EDGING

Abbreviations: K = knit; LH = left hand; P = pearl; sl = slip; st(s) = stitch(es); tog = together; yrn = yarn around needle; yfwd = yarn forward.

Cast on 25 st.
Knit one row.
Work in pattern as follows:
1st row Sl1, K2, P6, K3, yrn twice, K to end. 27 sts.
2nd row Yrn, K2tog, K11, P1, K to end.
3rd row Sl1, K2, P6, K to end.
4th row Yrn, K2tog, K to end.
5th row Sl1, K2, P6, K3, yrn twice, K2tog, yrn twice, K2tog, K to end. 29 sts.
6th row Yrn, K2tog, K10, P1, K2, P1, K to end.
7th row Sl1, K2, P6, K to end.
8th row Yrn, K2tog, K8, turn, K to end.
9th row Yrn, K2tog, K7, K2tog, K9, sl the 4th, 5th and 6th sts on LH needle over 1st, 2nd and 3rd sts, yfwd, K3, yfwd, K3. 27 sts.
10th row Sl1, K2, P6, K3, (yrn twice, K2tog) 3 times, K to end. 30 sts.
11th row Yrn, K2tog, K9, P1, K2, P1, K2, P1, K to end.
12th row Sl1, K2, P6, K to end
13th row Yrn, K2tog, K7, turn, K to end.
14th row Yrn, K2tog, K6, K2tog, K to end. 29 sts.

Lace edging on pincushion

15th row Sl1, K2, P6, K3, (yrn twice, K2tog) 4 times, K to end. 33 sts.
16th row Yrn, K2tog, K9 (P1, K2) 3 times, P1, K to end.
17th row Sl1, K2, P6, K15, sl all but last st over first st on LH needle, K2tog, 25 sts.
18th row Yrn, K2tog, K14, sl the 4th, 5th and 6th sts on LH needle over

1st, 2nd and 3rd sts, yrn, K3, yrn, K1, pick up loop between last st knitted and next st and K into back of it, K2. 25 sts.
Repeat 1st—18th rows 35 times more, or until the edging measures 1 m (39 in).
Cast off loosely leaving enough yarn to join row edges.

◐ MAKING THE PINCUSHION

Trim the embroidery, adding a 12 mm (½ in) seam allowance all around. Cut out the white cotton fabric (the backing) to the same size. From the ribbon, cut four 13 cm (5 in) lengths for the loops and four 15 cm (6 in) lengths for the tails. Fold the loops, place them on the right side of the pincushion, as shown in the diagram below, and tack (baste) to secure, stitching just inside the seamline. Repeat with the tails, keeping them in place in the same way. Trim the loose ends diagonally to prevent fraying.

Join together the short ends of the

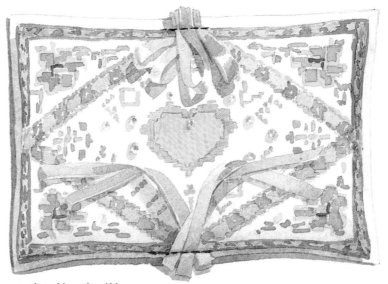

Attaching the ribbons

lace edging, overcasting the abutted edges to keep the joining flat. Run a gathering thread around the straight edge of the lace and pull up to fit the outside edge of the pincushion. With the right sides together, lay the lace on the embroidery over the ribbon trim with the scallops inside and the gathered edge just inside the seam allowance. Pin and tack (baste) the edge of the lace to the outer edge of the fabric (also inside the seamline), allowing extra fullness around the corners.

Place the backing fabric on top with the right sides together. Tack (baste) and machine stitch around, leaving a 9 cm (3½ in) opening along one short side. Remove the tacking (basting) stitches, trim back the seam, cut across the corners and turn the cover through to the right side. Stuff evenly with the loose wadding (batting) to a firm, rounded shape. Slipstitch the opening closed.

Decorate the outer and diamond-

Attaching the ribbon loops

Detail of tails on pincushion

shaped border with pins, if you like. Stitch single beads to each corner and at the points of the diamond.

Finally, gather the lace at the center of each side. Using white sewing thread and working from the wrong side, run gathering stitches across the width. Pull tightly and fasten off just on the edge of the pincushion.

⮑ ADAPTING THE BASIC PINCUSHION

Using the same basic techniques, make a traditional heart-shaped pincushion in a pretty pastel evenweave with plain white cross stitch embroidery.

The finished pincushion measures 18 cm × 18 cm (7 in × 7in) excluding the lace edging

⮑ MATERIALS
25 cm (10 in) square of pink linen, 25 threads to 2.5 cm (1 in)

Tacking (basting) thread
Tapestry needle size 26
Embroidery hoop (optional)
DMC 6-strand embroidery floss: see the thread list below
23 cm (9 in) of white Aida band with gold edging, 15 threads to 2.5 cm (1 in)
Small gold beads
1 × 20 g ball of white Coats Chain Mercer Crochet number 60 cotton yarn
1 pair of 2¾ mm (12) knitting needles
25 cm (10 in) square of pink cotton
Loose synthetic wadding (batting)
1 m (39 in) of pink satin ribbon, 6 mm (¼ in) wide
Matching sewing threads
Crewel needle size 7

⮑ THREAD LIST
	white
760	pink
3811	turquoise
	light gold thread

⮑ MAKING THE PINCUSHION
Following the color key, charts given opposite and the instructions for the basic pincushion, work the embroidery in the same way, and steam press on the wrong side. Pin and tack (baste) the band in place and, using turquoise 3811, secure it with small running stitches. Stitch the gold beads in place (see page 152) as shown on the chart. Knit the lace, and make up the pincushion as previously instructed.

PINCUSHION

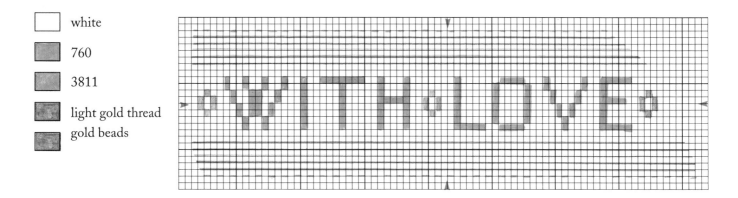

- white
- 760
- 3811
- light gold thread
- gold beads

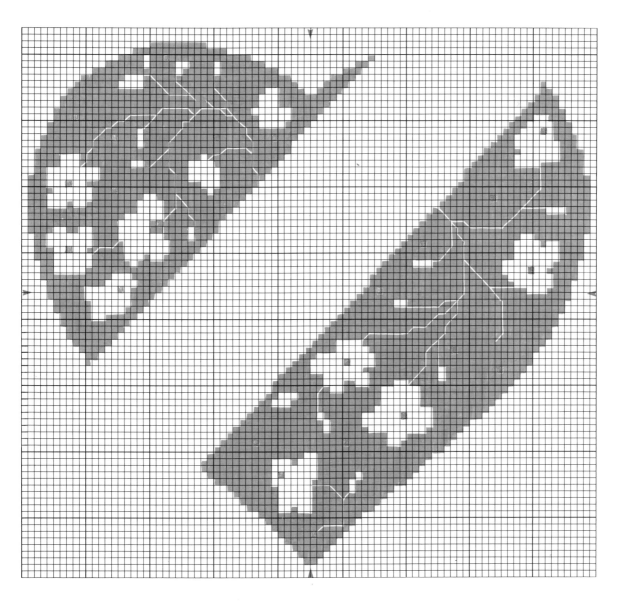

$\mathcal{A}$LPHABETS

Alphabet styles vary enormously, as seen in the flamboyant serifs and floral embellishments of the old German typeface used in the linen bag project on page 33, compared with the simple alphabet backstitched in single lines used on the new baby greeting card on page 111.

I have tried to use as wide a variety of alphabets as possible so that, in time and with a little practice, you should be able to chart your own mottoes and dedications to fit the space and fabric gauge of your choice.

Use the following alphabets to chart your own names and dates where required in the relevant projects.

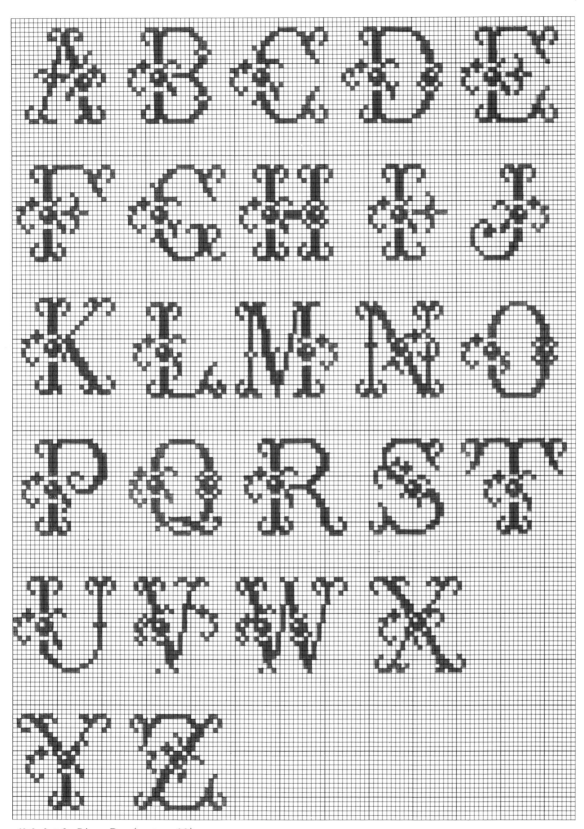

Alphabet for Linen Bag (see page 32)

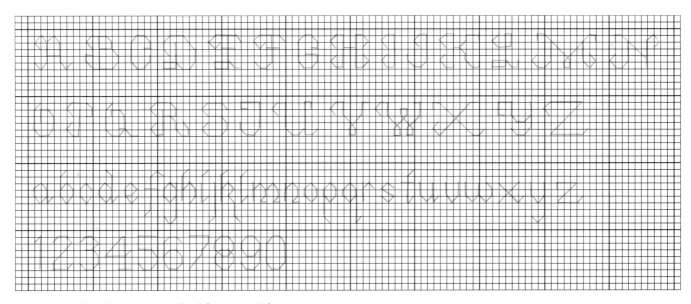

Alphabet for New Baby Greeting Card (see page 109)

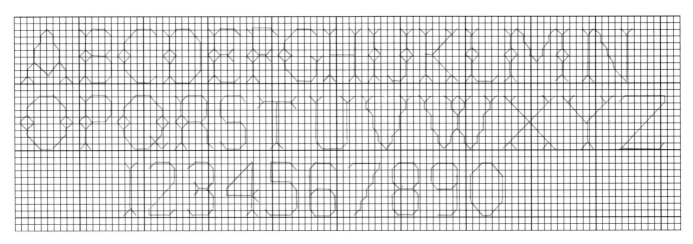

Alphabet for alternative New Baby Greeting Card (see page 112)

Alphabet for Pincushion (see page 134)

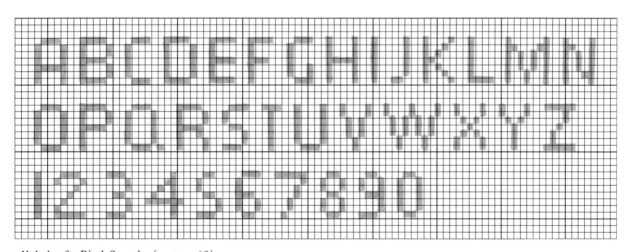

Alphabet for Birth Sampler (see page 68)

Alphabet for Initialed Bookmark (see page 131)

Alphabet for alternative Initialed Bookmark (see page 132)

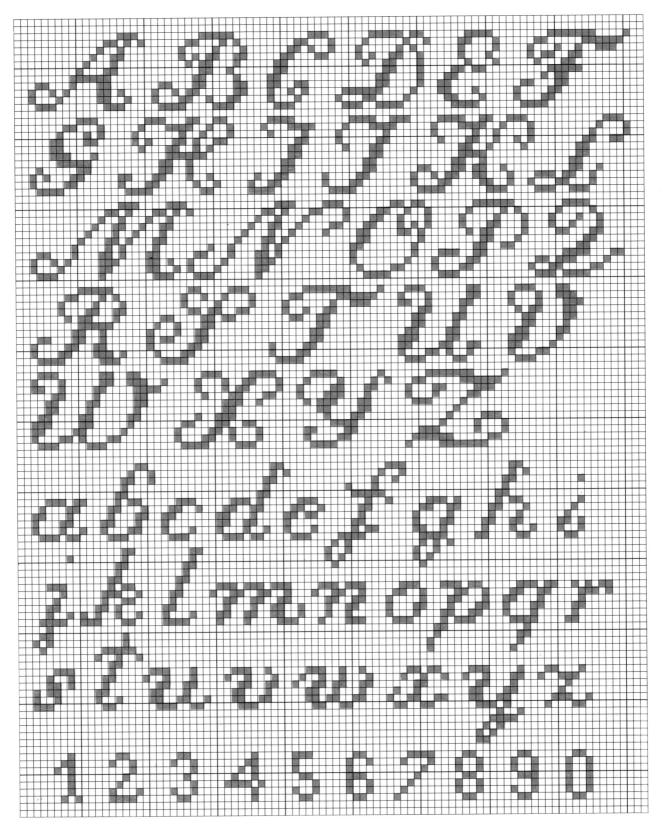

Alternative alphabet, provided to add variation in style

MATERIALS AND SKILLS

Over the next nine pages I have provided you with information and help, designed to make your embroidery easier to stitch and look even better when finished. All the basic materials for cross stitch are discussed here, together with fully illustrated techniques for every embroidery stitch and finish that is used in the projects in this book. Each project makes cross references to this section at the relevant points, but it would be equally valuable to read this section before beginning to sew.

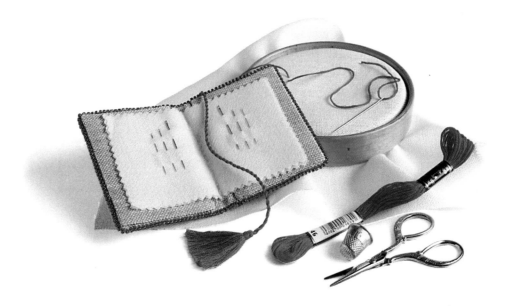

FABRICS

Cross stitch embroidery is easier to work on an evenweave fabric – that is, any fabric with the same number of threads counted in both directions, usually over 2.5 cm (1 in), when it is generally referred to as 14, 18, or 24 count, for example.

Linens are traditionally used for cross stitch embroidery around the world. They are available in a range of 'counts' and colors, although natural and antique finishes are more traditional. Due to the staple (fibre) and nature of the flax from which they are woven, some linens may have a pronounced uneven appearance.

Most linens are woven with a single weave with the exception of Hardanger, which has a double weave, and huckaback, which is woven in groups of threads (similar to cotton Aida) and forms a checked pattern. In addition to linens, evenweave fabrics are also made from cotton and linen mixes, such as Zweigart's Quaker Cloth which comes in a limited range of colors and counts; and pure cotton, such as Zweigart's Aida, Ainring, Lugana and Linda. These names signify the different counts and all come in a variety of colors.

The dressing given to these cotton fabrics makes them feel stiff and unyielding. On the one hand, the stiffness can help you to keep an even tension while stitching and will wash out with laundering, but on the other hand, you may prefer working with a softer fabric, so hand wash it before starting.

THREADS

Embroidery threads: Several types of embroidery thread can be used for cross stitching, including pearl threads and *coton à broder* but, for the projects given in this book, DMC six-strand embroidery floss has been used throughout. The exact number of strands used for each project is given with the instructions.

As a rule, fewer strands are used on finer fabrics and more strands on heavier fabrics. The overall aim, however, is to produce clearly defined stitches that cover the fabric well.

Tacking (basting) thread: This thread is a soft, loosely twisted cotton which is normally sold on large reels, and is cheaper to use than ordinary sewing thread. The advantages of using tacking (basting) thread are that it will not leave a mark when it has been pressed with an iron, whereas ordinary sewing thread often does. Should it get caught up while you are removing the stitches, it will break first rather than damage the fabric.

Sewing threads: These threads are tightly twisted, fine and yet strong. The most popular varieties are made from cotton or cotton/polyester mixes and come in a huge variety of colors.

NEEDLES

Round-ended tapestry needles should be used for cross stitching on evenweave fabrics. You will find that they move easily between the fabric intersections without piercing the ground threads. Tapestry needles are available in several sizes ranging from 18 to 26.

For making up the projects, you will also need a selection of Sharps needles for hand sewing.

For working additional surface embroidery such as the edge stitches on the child's pillow cover (see page 91), you will need crewel needles. These needles have sharp points and long oval eyes and are available in sizes 1-10.

FRAMES

A hoop or rectangular frame will keep the fabric evenly stretched while stitching. Although a frame for smaller pieces of embroidery is not essential, there are advantages to using one. When the fabric is supported in a frame, both hands are free to stitch – with one on top and one below – and many people find they eventually stitch faster and more evenly this way.

SCISSORS

It is important to use the right type of scissors for the job. For cutting out fabric, use sharp, dressmaker's shears. You will need a pair of small, sharp-pointed embroidery scissors for snipping into seams and neatening threads and, for cutting non-fabric items such as cardboard, cords and paper, a pair of general-purpose scissors.

SEWING MACHINE

A sewing machine is useful for making up items, especially for larger projects, where it will give a stronger seam and also help to speed up the finishing process.

GENERAL ACCESSORIES

In addition to the above-mentioned items, you will need stainless steel pins, a long ruler and pencil, a tape measure, an iron and ironing board, and a thimble for hand sewing, especially through bulky seams.

PREPARING THE FABRIC

Before cutting out, steam-press the fabric to remove all creases. Stubborn creases will be impossible to remove once they have been embroidered over so, if possible, avoid using that particular area of fabric. If colored fabrics are chosen for items you wish to launder, wash and press them first to test for colorfastness.

Always try to cut your fabric as economically as possible to avoid wasting fabric. Many evenweave fabrics, such as linen, fray very easily in the hand so, before you begin, it is a good idea to overcast the edges using tacking (basting) thread.

WORKING IN A HOOP

The hoop is most popular for working relatively small areas of embroidery. A hoop consists of two rings, usually made from wood, which fit closely one inside the other. The outer ring has a screw attachment so that the tension of the fabric can be adjusted and held firmly in place while the fabric is embroiderd.

Hoops are available in several sizes ranging from 10 cm (4 in) in diameter to very large quilting hoops measuring 60 cm (24 in) across. Hoops with table- or floor-stand attachments are also available.

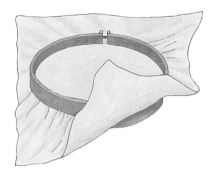

1 To stretch your fabric in a hoop, place the area to be embroidered over the inner ring and press the outer ring over it with the tension screw released.

2 Smooth the fabric and straighten the grain before tightening the tension screw attachment. The fabric should be evenly stretched.

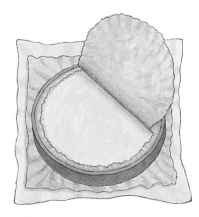

3 If wished, tissue paper can be placed between the outer ring and the embroidery, so that the hoop

does not mark the fabric. Tear away the paper to reveal the fabric, as shown.

4 Alternatively, before stretching your fabric in the hoop, bind both rings with bias binding, essentially to stop the fabric from slipping (some fine linens can slip badly) and also to prevent the rings from leaving pressure marks.

WORKING IN A RECTANGULAR FRAME

Rectangular frames are more popular for larger pieces of embroidery. They consist of two rollers with tapes attached, and two flat side pieces which slot into the rollers and are held in place by pegs or screw attachments.

These frames are measured by the length of the roller tape, and range in size from 30 cm (12 in) to 69 cm (27 in). They too, are available with or without adjustable table- or floor-stands.

As an alternative to this kind of frame, canvas stretchers and old picture frames of an appropriate size can be used, where the fabric edges are simply turned under and then secured with drawing pins (thumb tacks) or staples.

1 To stretch your fabric in a rectangular frame, cut out the fabric, allowing at least an extra 5 cm (2 in) all around the finished size of the embroidery. Tack (baste) a single 12 mm (½ in) hem on the top and bottom edges, and oversew 2.5 cm (1 in) wide tape to the other two sides. Mark the center both ways with tacking (basting) stitches.

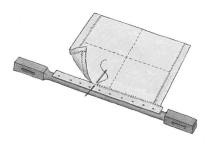

2 Working outward from the center, oversew the top and bottom edges to the roller tapes. Fit the side pieces into the slots, and roll any extra fabric onto one roller until it is taut.

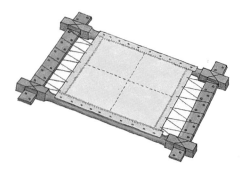

3 Insert the pegs or adjust the screw attachments to secure the frame. Thread a large-eyed needle (chenille needle) with strong thread and lace

both edges, securing the ends by winding them around the intersections of the frame. Lace the webbing at 2.5 cm (1 in) intervals, stretching the fabric evenly.

☞ CROSS STITCH

The following two methods of working are used for all cross-stitch embroidery. In each case, neat rows of stitches are produced on the wrong side of the fabric.

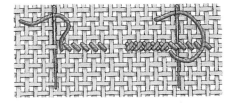

1 Work in horizontal rows when stitching large solid areas. Working from right to left, complete the first row of evenly-spaced diagonal stitches over the specific number of threads given in the project instructions. Then, working from left to right, repeat the process. Continue in this way, making sure that each stitch and successive rows cross in the same direction throughout the piece of embroidery.

2 When stitching diagonal lines, or individual groups of stitches, work downward, completing each stitch before moving to the next.

☞ BACKSTITCH

Backstitch is used in conjunction with cross stitch, sometimes for accompanying lettering but generally as an outline to emphasize a particular shape or shadow within a motif. The stitches are always worked over the same number of threads as the cross stitching to give uniformity to the finished embroidery. Use for continuous straight or diagonal lines.

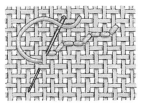

Bring out the needle on the right side of the fabric and make the first stitch from left to right; pass the needle behind the fabric, and bring it out one stitch length ahead towards the left. Repeat and continue in this way along the stitching line.

☞ BUTTONHOLE STITCH

Bring the needle out on the stitching line. Working from left to right, insert the needle above the stitchline (the required depth of the stitch away) and just to the right. Then take a downward stitch and bring it out

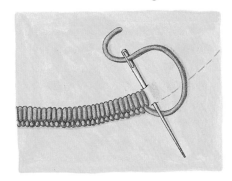

immediately below with the working thread under the needle. Tighten the loop and repeat to the end of the stitchline.

☞ TO MAKE A FRENCH KNOT
Bring the needle out where the knot is to be worked and, holding the thread down with the left thumb, wind the thread twice around the needle. Insert the needle close to the

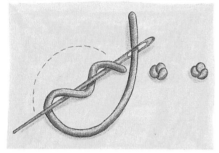

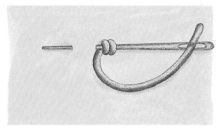

starting point and pull it through to the back of the embroidery so that a knot forms on the right side of the fabric, then fasten off the thread. If making more than one knot, do not fasten off; instead, reposition the needle for the next knot.

☞ STEMSTITCH
Bring out the needle on the stitchline and, working from left to right, make

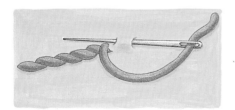

a stitch at a slight angle to the line. Continue in this way making sure that the thread always emerges in the middle of the previous stitch.

☞ HEMSTITCH
This is a decorative way of turning up a hem and is the traditional stitch used on table linen and bed linen. For best results, hemstitch should be worked on evenweave fabrics and fairly coarse weaves are the easiest to handle. Choose an embroidery thread similar in thickness to the fabric threads and use a tapestry needle to avoid piercing the fabric threads.

For a fringed finish, first remove a single thread at the hem and stitch along the line as shown. Complete the stitching and then remove the fabric threads below the hemstitching to make the fringing.

To secure a hem that has been turned up to the drawn-thread line and tacked (basted) in place, work from the right side and hemstitch as shown but, at the second stage of each

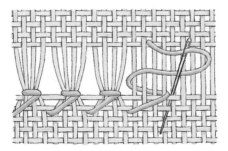

stitch, make sure the needle pierces the hem at the back of the fabric before pulling the thread through to repeat the stitch along the line.

Bring the needle out on the right side of the fabric two threads below

the drawn-thread line. Working from left to right, pick up either two or three threads, as shown in the diagram. Bring the needle out again and insert it behind the fabric, to emerge two threads down, ready to make the next stitch. Before reinserting the needle, pull the thread tight, so that the bound threads form a neat group.

☞ INSERTION STITCH
Tack (baste) the two edges to be joined with insertion stitch on to a backing. For the greeting card sachet (see page 103), fold in the corners, press and tack (baste) around through all layers. Secure the thread through the folded edge with one or two

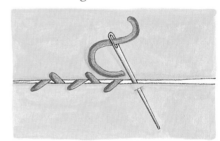

overstitches, then pass the needle diagonally behind the fold and bring it out a short distance away. Repeat on the opposite side, gently pulling the two edges together, and continue stitching alternate sides in this way.

☞ SLIPSTITCH
This is a nearly invisible stitch formed by slipping the thread under a fold of fabric. It can be used to join two folded edges, such as a cushion opening, or one folded edge to a flat surface.

Working from right to left, bring the needle and thread out through one

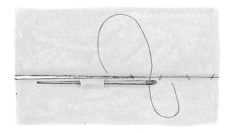

folded edge. For the first and each succeeding stitch, slip the needle through the fold of the opposite edge for about 6 mm (¼ in). Bring the needle out and continue to slip the needle alternately through the two folded edges.

⌒ HEMMING STITCH

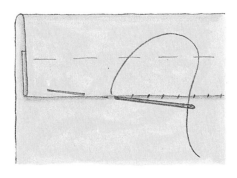

This small, almost invisible stitch can be used for all types of hems and for finishing edges which have been covered with a fabric binding.

Fold the hem or binding to the wrong side and pin or tack (baste) to secure. Using matching thread and holding the needle at an angle, make a tiny stitch in the fabric first; then insert it into the hem fold and make another small stitch. Pull the needle through and repeat along the stitchline, making the stitches of equal size and spacing them about 5 mm (³⁄₁₆ in) apart.

⌒ BLANKET STITCH

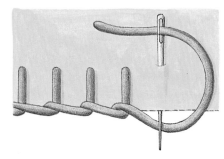

Working from left to right, bring the needle out on the stitchline (on the child's pillow cover, page 92, just below the seam). Hold the thread to the right and make a downward vertical stitch bringing the needle out over the thread. Repeat, inserting the needle a short distance away, about 6 mm (¼ in).

⌒ RUNNING STITCH

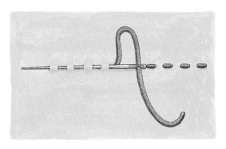

Working from right to left, take the needle in and out of the fabric at equal intervals, about 6 mm (¼ in) apart. Weave the needle in and out as many times as the fabric will permit before pulling the thread through.

⌒ HERRINGBONE STITCH

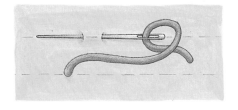

1 Placing the stitch centrally over the stitchline (on the child's pillow, page 92, over the seamline), bring the needle out about 6 mm (¼ in) below. Then insert the needle the same distance above the seamline and make a small stitch from right to left.

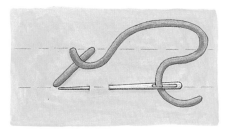

2 Take the thread over the worked stitch, and make a small stitch from right to left on the lower working line.

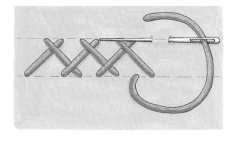

3 Continue in this way, working the stitches alternately on the upper and lower lines.

⌒ STITCHING ON BEADS
Bring out the needle in the appropriate place and thread on a bead. Insert the needle into the same hole, make a stitch underneath (the length of the bead) and bring it out

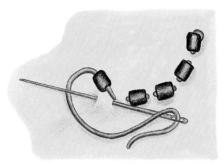

with the thread below the needle. Take the needle through to the back just beyond where it last emerged, then bring it out ready to attach the next bead.

☞ STITCHING ON SEQUINS WITH BEADS

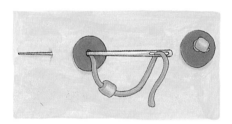

Bring the needle out through the eye of the sequin and thread on a small bead, then insert the needle back through the eye of the sequin and pull tight so that the bead rests firmly over the eye, securing the sequin.

☞ BUTTONHOLE LOOP

Run the needle through the folded edge of the fabric and secure the thread with one or two overstitches. Then make a loop (the width of the button) by taking a small stitch through the folded edge of the fabric, to the right, the required distance away. Take the needle back to the starting point making a second loop. Begin to work buttonhole stitch over the threads passing the needle

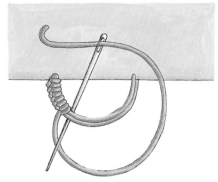

downwards and behind the loop, bringing it out with the thread below. Continue until the loop is covered and neatly fasten off the thread.

☞ STRAIGHT SEAMS

Unless otherwise stated, all seams are straight with a 1 cm ($^3/_8$ in) seam allowance, pressed open to finish.

1 After stitching the seam, finish off

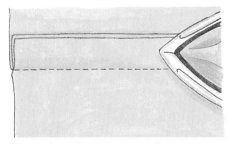

the ends and steam-press the seam allowance to one side, to press the stitches into the fabric.

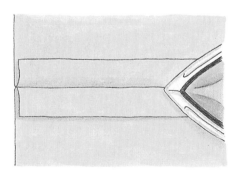

2 Press the seam allowances open. When you are making a project, remember to 'press as you sew' for best results.

☞ BIAS BINDING

Bias binding is a narrow strip of fabric cut across the grain to allow maximum 'give', and is an excellent covering for all edges, especially curved ones. It is available in three sizes: 12 mm ($^1/_2$ in), 2.5 cm (1 in) and 5 cm (2 in), and in a wide range of colors. Cotton lawn is by far the most popular (and practical) type, and is stocked by most needlework suppliers.

There are two methods of binding an edge: one-stage binding, where the binding is attached by stitching through all layers, and two-stage binding, where it is attached in two stages so that the stitching cannot be seen on the right side.

For one-stage binding, using double-folded binding, encase the raw edge with the binding and tack (baste) in place.

Working from the right side, machine stitch along the edge, through all layers, so that both sides are stitched at the same time.

1 For two-stage binding, open out the fold on one edge of the binding and pin it in position on the fabric, right sides together, matching the

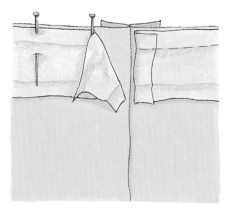

foldline to the seamline. Fold over the cut end of the binding. Overlap the starting point by about 12 mm (½ in). Tack (baste) and machine stitch along the seamline.

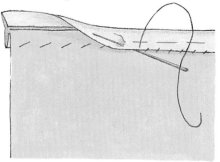

2 Fold the binding over the raw edge to the wrong side and tack (baste) in place. Using matching thread, hem to finish. Take the hemming stitches through the previously made stitches or place within the seam allowance to prevent them from showing.

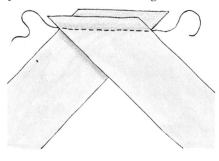

To join bias binding, cut the strips across the straight grain. Place them right sides together, pin and stitch across, and then press the seam open.

MAKING A TWISTED CORD

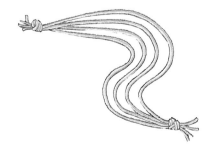

1 Use a variety of yarns to achieve different effects and vary the number of strands for different weights of cord. Take the required number of strands, cut to three times the length of the finished cord and knot each end.

2 Fasten one end of the cord around a door handle, hold it in a drawer or slip it over a pencil and anchor in a convenient place. Holding the strands taut, rotate until the strands are tightly twisted.

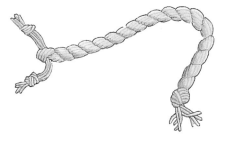

3 Fold in half at the center and knot the ends together. Holding the knot, give the cord a sharp shake and even out the twists by smoothing the cord from the knotted end. Reknot at the fold and cut to make a neat tassel.

ATTACHING A DECORATIVE CORD

To attach a fine- to medium-weight cord, simply slip one cut end into the seam – leave a 2 cm (¾ in) gap in the seam – and secure with matching thread. Slipstitch the cord around the edge of the cushion, alternately catching the underside of the cord and sliding the needle under a few threads of the seam so that the finished stitching is completely hidden.

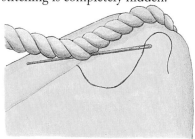

Finish with the two ends neatly tucked into the seam; cross them smoothly and secure with a few well-hidden stitches. Secure the seam opening in the same way.

MAKING A TASSEL

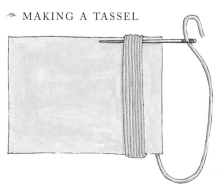

1 Make a very simple tassel by winding the appropriate embroidery or sewing thread around a small piece of cardboard about 3 cm (1¼ in) wide. Thread the loose end into a needle, slip the tassel threads off the card and wind the loose thread several times round them, close to the top.

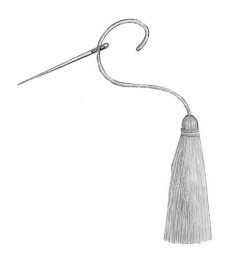

2 Pass the needle up through the bound threads and bring it out at the top of the tassel, ready to be sewn in place. Cut through the loops to finish.

☞ CUSHION TIES

Fabric ties, arranged singly or as a pair of bows, can be a decorative feature in themselves. Used to close a placket opening across the center back of the cushion cover, the ties should be about 2.5 cm (1 in) wide and 30 cm (12 in) long.

1 For medium-weight fabrics, fold the fabric lengthwise in half right sides facing, pin and machine stitch around two sides. Trim across the corners.

2 Using the blunt end of a knitting needle placed in the seam at the short end, turn the tie to the right side. Gradually ease the fabric over the end of the needle while pushing it

through the fabric. Push out the corners and press the tie flat. Repeat for the remaining ties.

☞ MITERING CORNERS

There are several types of miter, but in each case the purpose is essentially to reduce bulk and to make the corner neat and square.

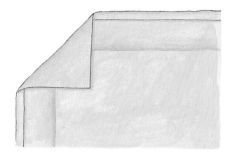

1 To miter a corner, first plan the depth of the hem and allow an extra 6 mm (^{1}/4 in) for folding. Fold over the corner as shown in the diagram and finger-press the creaseline.

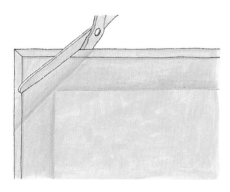

2 Allow a further 6 mm (^{1}/4 in) beyond this line and cut across.

3 Fold the fabric with the two outer edges together and machine stitch across, taking a 6mm (^{1}/4 in) seam and stopping at the creased line of the hem.

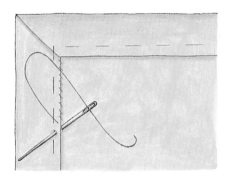

4 Press the seam open and turn the corner to the right side. Either turn under the hem, tack (baste) and hem on the wrong side, or finish the hem following the instructions given with the project.

⌒ MOUNTING EMBROIDERY
Embroidered pictures look best if they are first stretched over cardboard before framing under glass. A thin layer of wadding (batting) is placed between the fabric and the cardboard to give opaqueness and some protection to the corners and outer edges. Most fabrics used for cross stitch are fairly lightweight and can be attached at the back with pieces of masking tape, but heavier fabrics are best laced across the back with strong thread.

The cardboard should be cut to the size of the finished embroidery with at least an extra 6 mm (1/4 in) added all around to allow for the recess in the picture frame.

Using a pencil, mark the center both ways on the cardboard. Mark the center of the wadding (batting) by placing pins in the middle of the outer edges. Lay the embroidery face down, center the wadding (batting) on top and then the cardboard, aligning pencil marks, pins and tacking (basting). Remove the pins.

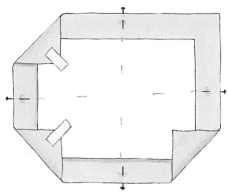

1 To attach the fabric with masking tape, begin by folding over the fabric at each corner and securing it with small pieces of masking tape.

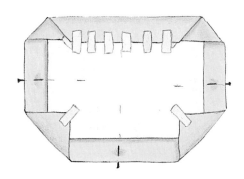

2 Working first on one side and then on the opposite side, fold over the fabric on all sides and secure it firmly with more pieces of masking tape, placed about 2.5 cm (1 in) apart. Check occasionally to see that the design is centered, and adjust the masking tape, if necessary. Neaten the mitered corners also with masking tape, pulling the fabric firmly to give a smooth, even finish. Overstitch the mitered corners, if necessary.

To attach the fabric by lacing, lay the embroidery face down with the wadding (batting) and cardboard centered on top, as shown in the

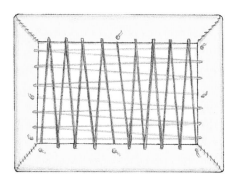

diagram. Begin with the corners, as shown, and also fold over the fabric on opposite sides, mitering the folds at the corners. Using strong thread knotted at one end and beginning in the middle of one side, lace across the

two edges. Repeat on the other two sides. Finally, pull up the stitches fairly tightly to stretch the fabric evenly over the cardboard, periodically checking to see that your design is still centered. Adjust if necessary. Overstitch the mitered corners to finish.

SUPPLIERS

I have used DMC threads and Zweigart fabrics throughout this book. These materials are available in many craft and fabric stores throughout North America. If you are unable to locate a supplier, contact the following addresses.

For information about DMC products:

DMC Corporation
10 Port Kearny
South Kearny, NJ 07032

To mail-order DMC products:

Herrschers
800/441-0838

For Zweigart products:

Needleworker's Delight
100 Claridge Place
Colonia, NJ 07067
800/931-4545

Presentation cards may be mail-ordered from:

Willmaur Crafts Corporation
735 Old York Road
Willow Grove, PA 19090
215/659-8702

Yarn Tree Designs, Inc.
P.O. Box 724
Ames, IA 50010
515/232-3121

BIBLIOGRAPHY

A Creative Guide to Cross Stitch Embroidery, Jan Eaton (New Holland, paperback 1993)

A Sampler of Alphabets (Sterling Publishing Co., 1987)

Around the World in Cross Stitch, Jan Eaton (New Holland, 1992)

The Cross Stitch and Sampler Book (Methuen, 1985)

Cross Stitch for Children, Dorothea Hall (Merehurst, 1992)

Cross Stitch for Special Occasions, Dorothea Hall (Merehurst, 1992)

Cross Stitch for the Home, Dorothea Hall (Merehurst, 1992)

Embroidery, Mary Gostelow (Marshall Cavendish Editions, 1977)

Embroidery Studio, The Embroiderers' Guild (David & Charles, 1993)

Fairy Tales in Cross Stitch Dorothea Hall (Merehurst, 1992)

Flowers in Cross Stitch, Shirley Watts (Merehurst, 1994)

Glorious Inspiration, Kaffe Fasset (Century, 1991)

Inspiration in Cross Stitch, Dorothea Hall (Storey Publishing, 1995)

Making Your Own Cross Stitch Gifts, Sheila Coulson (Storey Publishing, 1994)

Nursery Rhymes in Cross Stitch Dorothea Hall (Merehurst, 1991)

Quick and Easy Cross Stitch, Dorothea Hall (Merehurst, 1992)

Traditional Samplers, Sarah Don (David & Charles, 1986)

Treasures from the Embroiderers' Guild Collection (David & Charles, 1991)

ACKNOWLEDGMENTS

Special thanks to my son, Jonathan, for his editorial assistance and support over the past few months.

I would also like to extend grateful thanks to the following people who have helped with cross stitching the designs, and who were always ready to share my enthusiasm with skill and understanding.

Christina Eustace

Janet Grey

Kerri Laver

Penny Laver

Judith Maurer

Helen Milo

Janey Oak

Mary Walter

Thanks must also go to Cara Ackerman of DMC Creative World, who helped in many ways, and supplied various evenweave fabrics and threads. Finally, to Alan Gray of Framecraft Miniatures Ltd. who kindly supplied the greeting card mounts.

INDEX